官方授权

STEP BY STEP 听懂
CNN 财经评论

CNN Business Comments

LiveABC 编著

科学出版社
北京

图书在版编目（CIP）数据

Step by Step 听懂CNN财经评论 / LiveABC 编著.--北京：科学出版社，
2013.1
　（CNN互动英语系列）
　ISBN 978-7-03-035683-3

　I. ①S… II. ①L… III. ①经济-英语-听说教学-自学参考资料 IV.
①H319.9

　中国版本图书馆CIP数据核字（2012）第231795号

责任编辑：刘彦慧 / 责任校对：朱光光
责任印制：赵德静 / 封面设计：无极书装
联系电话：010-64019074/电子邮箱：liuyanhui@mail.sciencep.com

科学出版社 出版
北京东黄城根北街16号
邮政编码：100717
http://www.sciencep.com
北京佳信达欣艺术印刷有限公司 印刷
科学出版社发行 各地新华书店经销

*

2013年1月第 一 版　开本：B5（720×1000）
2013年1月第一次印刷　印张：15 1/2
字数：420 000

定价：66.00元

（含DVD互动光盘1张）

（如有印装质量问题，我社负责调换）

听懂英语新闻，与国际接轨的最佳选择！

学了这么多年英语，想看看英语新闻却觉得很吃力？看着新闻画面似乎不难猜出主要事件，但对于新闻细节却像是"鸭子听雷——听了也不动（懂）"？其实主要原因在于大多数人"听"英语的能力比阅读能力差，再加上不了解相关背景或专有名词、跟不上新闻播报速度等，于是就对收听英语新闻产生了却步情绪。

收听国际英语新闻是与国际接轨、掌握时事脉动的最佳方式，而 CNN 是最具国际知名度的新闻媒体之一。本书内容均取材自 CNN 电视新闻网，对于想提高英语能力及职场竞争力，掌握财经脉动，拓宽视野，吸收新知的读者来说，本书是您最佳的选择。

本书精选 26 篇报道，依主题分为以下五大部分：

◆ 行业之道
◆ 品牌哲学
◆ 财经内幕
◆ 商海拾趣
◆ 环球生活

全书的新闻报道采用中英文对照的方式，而且给出了单词与重要短语解析，并补充了相关词汇及延伸用法，同时针对主题内容扩展了各种相关知识。

随书附赠电脑互动光盘。读者可以利运用多媒体技术将文字（text）、影像（image）、声音（sound）结合在一起，加深学习印象、增进学习效率。针对苦于跟不上英语新闻速度的读者们，互动光盘中还在正常速度的原音 MP3 之外附有慢速的朗读 MP3。慢速语音由专业外教录制，发音清晰，方便您循序渐进，由慢至快地理解新闻内容。

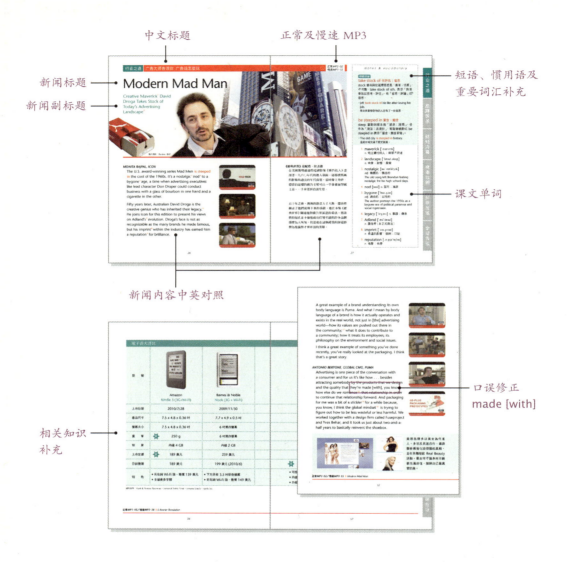

希望读者能通过本书专业的新闻报道学习到老外最常用的英语单词、短语用法及口语表达，并循序渐进地锻炼听力、培养语感。相信这会是您精通英文的最佳途径！

目　录

行业之道 1

品牌哲学 45

商海拾趣　　149

环球生活 189

光盘使用方法

★ 系统建议需求

[硬件]

* Pentium 4 以上处理器（或同等 AMD、Celeron 处理器）

* 512 MB 内存

* 屏幕分辨率 1024 * 768 像素以上

* 硬盘需求空间 200 MB

* 16 倍速以上光驱

* 声卡、扬声器及麦克风（内置或外接）

[软件]

* Microsoft Windows XP、VISTA、Windows 7 简体中文版系统

* Microsoft Windows Media Player 9 以上

* Adobe Flash Player 10 以上

★ 请注意！

◎ 出于对版权的保护，本光盘只能在电脑上带盘运行，无法将光盘内容复制到电脑硬盘上再进行安装。

◎ 如果您的电脑装有 360 软件，请在安装光盘之前先关闭所有与 360 相关的软件，包括 360 杀毒软件、360 安全卫士、360 浏览器等。

◎ 在 Vista 系统中，安装互动光盘如遇到以下问题：

* 出现"安装字体错误"的信息。
* 出现"无法安装语音识别"的信息。

请运行以下步骤：
步骤一：删除该产品；
步骤二：进入控制面板；
步骤三：点击"用户账户"选项；

步骤四：点击"开启或关闭用户账户控制"；
步骤五：将"使用（用户账户控制）UAC 来协助保护您的电脑"选项取消勾选；
步骤六：再次运行安装光盘。

◎ 在 Windows 7 系统中，安装互动光盘如遇到以下问题：

* 出现"安装字体错误"的信息。
* 出现"无法安装语音识别"的信息。

请运行以下步骤：
步骤一：进入控制面板，打开"程序"，进入"程序和功能"，卸载该产品；
步骤二：进入控制面板，点击"用户账户和家庭安全"选项；
步骤三：再点击"用户账户"；
步骤四：点击"更改用户账户控制设置"；
步骤五：将滑动条拖至最底端（"从不通知"的位置）；
步骤六：点击"确定"后，需重新启动电脑；
步骤七：再次运行安装光盘。

★ 光盘安装程序介绍

步骤一：进入中文操作系统。

步骤二：将光盘放进光驱。

步骤三：本产品具备 Auto Run 自动运行功能，如果您的电脑支持此功能，则将自动出现"CNN 互动英语系列——Step by Step 听懂 CNN 财经评论"的安装界面。

1. 如果您的电脑已安装过本系列任意产品，您可以直接点击"快速安装"图标，进行快速安装；否则请点击"安装"图标，进行完整安装。

2. 如果您的电脑不支持 Auto Run 光盘自动播放功能，请打开 Windows "我的电脑"，点击光驱，并运行光盘根目录下的 autorun.exe 程序。

3. 如果运行 autorun.exe 仍然无法安装，请进入本光盘的 setup 文件夹，运行 setup.exe 程序，即可进行安装。

4. 如果您要删除"CNN 互动英语系列——Step by Step 听懂 CNN 财经评论"，请点击"开始"，选择"设置"，选择"控制面板"，选择"添加或删除程序"，在菜单中点击"CNN 互动英语系列——Step by Step 听懂 CNN 财经评论"，并运行"更改 / 删除"即可。

5. 当语音识别系统或录音功能无法使用时，请检查声卡驱动程序是否正常，并确认硬盘空间足够且 Windows 录音程序可以使用。

★ 光盘操作说明

光盘安装后点击"运行"，即进入本光盘的学习内容。按顺序说明如下：

◎主画面

主画面说明：

1. 主画面共有 10 个图标，分别为：行业之道、品牌哲学、财经内幕、商海拾趣、环球生活、听力大考验、索引、说明、科学出版社及退出。

2. 点击"行业之道"、"品牌哲学"、"财经内幕"、"商海拾趣"、"环球生活"课程图标，将于屏幕中出现其中的单元名称，点击后即可进入该单元课程。

◎ 影片学习

影片学习工具栏说明：

1. 画面右侧由上至下依次为：自动播放、播放／暂停、播下一句、播上一句、反复播放本句、全屏幕播放及设置。

2. 画面左侧由上至下依次为：目录、上一篇、下一篇、单词解释、文字学习、主画面、退出。

3. 画面下方是英文及中文字幕，通过点击字幕前的图标，可以选择出现或隐藏字幕，便于做听力练习。

4. 点击"自动播放"图标，则自动由第一个影片开始播放。

5. 字幕上方有一个影片播放点控制栏，可决定影片播放的起点。

6. 点击"Setting"图标可调整反复播放、音量大小的设置。

◎ 文字学习

在影片学习中，点击"文字学习"图标，即可进入本画面。

文字学习工具栏说明：

听力练习

点击"听力练习"图标，电脑会自动朗读本段的内容，但不会显示出中、英文。

全文朗读

点击"全文朗读"图标，电脑会自动朗读本段新闻的内容。

角色扮演

点击"角色扮演"图标，则会在图标左侧出现人名。此时，您可选择要扮演的角色，程序将关闭该角色的声音，由您和电脑进行对话练习，当您的发音不正确时，则会出现一个对话框，您可以选择"再读一次"、"略过"或"读给我听"来完成或跳过该句对话；也可以调整语音识别的灵敏度。若您的发音正确，则对话会一直进行下去。

快慢朗读

当您觉得对话速度太快时，可以点击"快慢朗读"图标，再点击"全文朗读"图标或任意句子，朗读速度将变慢，让您听得更清楚。若您开始觉得速度太慢，想恢复一般速度，只要再

次点击"快慢朗读"图标，即可恢复成一般速度。

反复朗读

点击"反复朗读"图标后，再点击任意句子，即反复播放该句。

中文翻译

点击"中文翻译"图标后，画面下方将出现中文翻译框，您可在中文翻译框内看到课文的中文翻译。若您点击中文翻译框中的某句中文，则会朗读相对应的英文句子；同样，点击正文中的任意英文句子，也会朗读该句英文，并标示出其中文翻译。

（当反蓝字无法使用重复或慢速朗读功能时，请开启中文翻译功能后，再次点击即可。）

录音

1. 点击"录音"图标后，开启录音功能控制栏，截图如下。

2. 按键功能由左至右为：全选、录音／停止、播放／暂停以及播放影片声音。点击最左方的"全选"图标，会出现全部句子录音；若您只想选择某段正文，只要在该段前方的方框（□）点击一下即可。若您点击最右方的"播放影片声音"图标，则在您进行录音或播放录音前，都将播放该段的影片原声。

3. 录音步骤如下：

  (1) 先点击您要进行录音的句子，并选择是

否要在录音前播放原声。

(2) 点击"录音"键。

(3) 请在电脑播放完原声后,对着麦克风读出您所点击的句子。

(4) 当您完成该句录音后,请按键盘上的"空格键",结束录音。

(5) 点击"播放"键,即可听到您所录的声音。

4. 点击左方的"Speech Recognition"图标,将启动"语音识别"功能,请依照以下步骤进行语音识别:

(1) 先选择要进行语音识别的句子,并选择是否要在语音识别前播放原声。

(2) 点击"Speech Recognition"图标。

(3) 画面出现"请录音"时,请对着麦克风读出您点击的句子,如果您的发音正确,则将继续进行下一句;如果发音不正确,则会出现一个对话框,您可选择"再读一次"、"略过"或"读给我听"来完成或跳过该句对话;也可在此调整语音识别的灵敏度。

5. 当您要在中途结束录音或语音识别时,请在任意处点击一下即可结束该功能。

词 典

当您点击"词典"图标后,在画面下方将出现词典框,此时点击课文中的任意单词,词典框内会出现该单词的音标及中文翻译,并读出该词发音。

打 印

当您点击"打印"图标后,在画面下方将出现打印控制键。您可选择"全部打印"或"部分打印";打印内容可选择是否包括中文翻译。此外,本光盘还提供存盘功能,您可以选择全部储存或部分储存;并选择是否储存中文翻译。

说 明

当您点击"说明"图标时,即会进入辅助说明页。您可借此了解本光盘内容的各项操作说明及用法。

设 置

若您想多次收听朗读,选取"设置"图标,将出现一个控制视窗,您可在此设置反复的间隔秒数及句子的反复次数,也可在此调整播放音量大小。

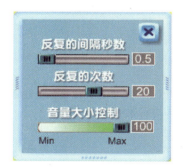

点击"加入自选单词"图标后,您可以点击您要记录的单词。

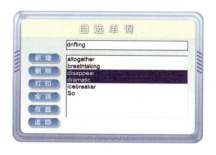

在此,您可以进行单词学习也可以删除或打印任意单词。

单词解释

列出本场景的重点单词（词性、音标、中文解释），点击该单词会发声。

学习重点

如：Northwest Passage.

当您在点击文中蓝色字体的学习重点时，画面下方会出现说明框，并有发音；若在开启"中文翻译"功能时点击，则朗读您点击的句子。

段落朗读

如：Bear Grylls, Adventurer:

当您点击文中的人名时，程序将自动朗读此人的该段会话。

◎ **索引**

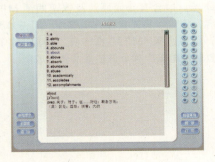

索引说明：

1. 在主画面点击"索引"图标，进入索引画面，其中包括单词及学习重点索引。

2. 单词：

   （1）在此将所有的单词按字母分类，点击单词会出现该单词的音标、中文翻译及发音。

   （2）连续点击单词两次或点击"例句显示"图标，即会出现该单词的课文例句。

   （3）连续点击例句两次或点击"连接课文"图标，即跳至该例句的"文字学习"画面。

   （4）点击"自选单词"图标，您可以在此看到您在学习过程中加入的自选单词。

   （5）点击"朗读"图标，则会将所选字母的单词从头到尾读一次；点击"打印"图标，则将以该字母开头的所有单词打印出来。

   （6）点击任意单词后，再点击"打印"图标，可打印该单词的内容。

3. 学习重点：

   （1）在此列出本光盘所有课程的学习重点。用鼠标点击任意学习重点，会自动朗读。

   （2）连续点击两次或点击"连接课文"图标，即跳至该学习重点的"文字学习"画面。

   （3）点击"返回"图标，则回到单词检索画面。

   （4）点击"朗读"图标，则会将所有的词语从头到尾读一次；点击"打印"图标，则将所有的学习重点打印出来。

◎ 听力大考验

1. 听力填空：

（1）点击画面右方的"播放键"即可听到该题的声音，请逐一填入正确答案。

（2）上方的进度将提示您目前正进行到第几题，完成题目后请点击"下一题"图标，继续进行测验。

（3）完成所有的题组后，请点击"交卷"图标，进行评估，点击"查看内容"图标即可查阅该次测验的答题过程；也可点击"再试一次"重新进行评估。

（4）点击"放弃作答"图标，将退出测验画面并不记录答题过程。

2. 听力理解：

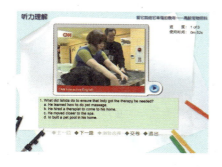

（1）点击画面右方的播放键即可听到该段影片的声音，请选择正确答案。

（2）上方的进度将提示您目前正进行到第几题，完成题目后请点击"下一题"图标，继续进行测验。

（3）完成所有的题组后，请点击"交卷"图标，进行评估，点击"查看内容"图标即可查阅该次测验的答题过程；也可点击"再试一次"重新进行评估。

（4）点击"放弃作答"图标，将退出测验画面并不记录答题过程。

◎ 说明

1. 在主画面点击"说明"图标，在此提供"操作说明"及"语音识别设置说明"。

2. 您可了解本光盘内容的各项操作说明、用法及语音识别设置上的安装说明。

◎ 科学出版社

点击本图标，将连接到科学出版社官方网站。

★ 原文朗读 MP3

互动光盘中含有新闻原声及慢速朗读 MP3 内容，您可以将光盘放在电脑中，打开本光盘，从中选择"MP3"文件夹，将里面的内容复制到电脑中或者其他播放器中收听。

CNN
Business Comments

行业之道

Modern Mad Man

Creative Maverick[1] David Droga Takes Stock of Today's Advertising Landscape[2]

图片提供：Reuters 杂志

MONITA RAJPAL, ICON

The U.S. award-winning series *Mad Men* is steeped in the cool of the 1960s. It's a nostalgic[3] nod[4] to a bygone[5] age, a time when advertising executives like lead character Don Draper could conduct business with a glass of bourbon in one hand and a cigarette in the other.

Fifty years later, Australian David Droga is the creative genius who has inherited their legacy.[6] He joins *Icon* for this edition to present his views on Adland's[7] evolution. Droga's face is not as recognizable as the many brands he made famous, but his imprint[8] within the industry has earned him a reputation[9] for brilliance.

❶ 广告大师告诉你——广告该怎么 "玩"

Notes & Vocabulary

标题扫描

take stock of 作评估；反思

stock 当名词在这里意思是 "衡量；估算"，不可数，take stock of sth. 表示 "对某事加以思考、评估"，有 "反思；评论" 的意思。

· Jeff **took stock of** his life after losing his job.
杰夫失业后对他的人生有了一些反思。

be steeped in 富含；饱含

steep 当动词原本指 "浸泡；浸润"，引申为 "浸淫；沉浸于"，常写成被动式 be steeped in 表示 "富含、饱含某物"。

· The old city **is steeped in** history.
这座古城充满了历史气息。

1. **maverick** [ˈmævrɪk]
   n. 特立独行的人；与众不同者

2. **landscape** [ˈlændˌskep]
   n. 风景；状态；风貌

3. **nostalgic** [nɑˈstældʒɪk]
   adj. 怀旧的；怀念的
   The old song left Brandon feeling nostalgic for his high school days.

4. **nod** [nɑd] *n.* 认可；准许

5. **bygone** [ˈbaɪˌgɔn]
   adj. 过去的；以往的
   The author portrays the 1950s as a bygone era of political paranoia and social repression.

6. **legacy** [ˈlɛgəsɪ] *n.* 事迹；传承

7. **Adland** [ˈædˌlænd]
   n. 广告界（非正式用法）

8. **imprint** [ˈɪmˌprɪnt]
   n. 长远的影响；铭刻；印记

9. **reputation** [ˌrɛpjəˈteʃən]
   n. 名声；名誉

《经典世界》莫妮塔·拉吉波

获奖连连的美国电视连续剧《广告狂人》中充斥着 20 世纪 60 年代的迷人元素。这部怀旧风格的连续剧在向过去的年代致意。当时像主角唐·德雷伯这样的广告主管可以一手拿着波旁威士忌，一手拿着烟洽谈生意。

50 年之后，澳大利亚的创意天才大卫·德洛格继承了他们的传统。他在本集《经典世界》里阐述他对广告界演进的看法。德洛格的面孔并不像他打响的许多品牌那么广为人知，但是他在这个产业里的深远影响为他赢得了 "才华横溢" 这一美誉。

Droga has won more awards than anyone else in history at the industry's biggest event, the Cannes Lions Advertising Festival. After an exceptional career at Saatchi and Saatchi Asia, London and as chief creative officer for Publicis, Droga founded his own company where an audacious[10] campaign[11] set the tone[12] for his attempt to redefine[13] the ad game.

DAVID DROGA, FOUNDER AND CREATIVE CHAIRMAN, DROGA5

Actually, the very first thing we launched[14] our agency on four years ago was a launch for Mark Ecko, the youth fashion brand. Mark Ecko built his billion-dollar empire from his garage where he started life as a graffiti[15] artist.

In graffiti culture it's all about what they call the "heavenly sites," which is the harder the place to put your graffiti, the more respect. And we released a film that seemed like some people had broken into Andrews Air Force Base and sprayed graffiti on Air Force One. But instead of just putting it out[16] as a regular commercial,[17] we launched it anonymously[18] to all his most hard-core[19] fans, and they're the ones who actually pushed it out[20] to the national media.

Advertising doesn't have to be pollution, advertising can be amazing. Advertising can contribute to culture. Advertising can lead culture. Advertising can solve social issues. You know, advertising is this

德洛格在广告界最大的盛事戛纳广告节得过的奖比任何人都多。他在萨奇广告亚洲与伦敦分公司的从业生涯中表现优异，还在阳狮集团当过创意总监。之后他创立了自己的公司，并以一个大胆的营销广告展现出他要重新定义广告玩法的风格。

Droga5 创办人兼创意总监 大卫·德洛格

实际上，四年前我们的公司开始运作，做的第一个广告是马克·艾柯，一个年轻的时尚品牌。其创始人马克·艾柯原本是一个从自家车库起家的涂鸦艺术家，他在车库里打造了他的亿元帝国。

在涂鸦文化中，他们有所谓的"天堂地点"，是指在越难操作的地方涂鸦就越受人尊敬。在我们发布的影片中像是有些人闯入了安德鲁空军基地，并在空军一号上涂鸦。但我们并未把这段影片当做一般的广告推出，而是匿名发布给了马克·艾柯最忠实的粉丝们，实际上是他们把这段影片推上了国内媒体。

广告不一定是污染，广告可以是令人惊奇的。广告可以对文化有所贡献。广告可以引导文化。广告可以解决社会问题。你知道，广告是拥有许多触角的产业，可以借此发挥

Notes & Vocabulary

10. **audacious** [ɔˋdeʃəs]
adj. 大胆的；冒险的
The talk show guest made several audacious claims about the government.

11. **campaign** [ˌkæmˋpen]
n. （商业、政治、社会活动等）宣传活动；造势活动

12. **set the tone (for)**
定调；设定风格、气氛等
The opening speaker's light-hearted remarks set the tone for the evening.

13. **redefine** [ˌridɪˋfaɪn] *v.* 重新定义
Filmmakers of the French New Wave redefined the role of the director.

14. **launch** [lɔntʃ] *v.* 发起；发动
The clothing brand launched its fall line at the Paris fashion show.

15. **graffiti** [grəˋfiti] *n.* 涂鸦

16. **put sth. out** 生产；推出；出版
The record label put out several hit singles in the 1960s.

17. **commercial** [kəˋmɜʃəl]
n. （电视或电台）广告

18. **anonymously** [əˋnɑnəməslɪ]
adv. 匿名地

19. **hard-core** [ˌhɑrdˋkɔr]
adj. 死忠的；死硬派的
Bill is a hard-core sports fan.

20. **push sth. out** 推展；推广
Development of the town soon pushed out into the surrounding countryside.

industry that has so many tentacles[21] and it can do great things with those. And it's more than just go through the motions and bombard[22] you into submission.[23]

I think where it's changed drastically for us and for brands is we're no longer just start and finish story tellers. We instigate[24] stories so we can create these brand stories, but really at the same time we move from being creators to curators.[25] Essentially we may create the beginning of a story, but then really we hand it over to the consumers and let them take ownership of it.

Proof that the advertising landscape is changing is you're seeing a lot of big billion-dollar brands actually having a more honest relationship and being a lot more transparent,[26] which is only a good thing. I think a wonderful example of this [is] the Dove "Real Beauty" campaign.

I think in a huge category[27] where billions and billions of dollars are spent every year making everyone look glamorous[28] and beautiful— unrealistically[29] beautiful—Dove called them out[30] and they went behind the scenes to show what real beauty is. It was a bold move, some would have said it was a risky move, but the fact that the consumers themselves responded in droves[31] is only proof that consumers want to have a more authentic[32] relationship.

很好的影响力。广告不只是触动情感，把你轰炸到投降而已。

我想，对我们和品牌而言，最大的改变是我们不再是讲故事并总结故事的人。我们开启故事，因此我们可以创造品牌故事，但在同时，我们从创作者变成策划者。基本上，我们可能会创造故事的开端，但是接着就把它们交给消费者，让他们自行把故事发展下去。

广告业正在改变的一个证据，就是你看到许多大资本额的品牌对消费者更诚实、更坦承了，这是件很棒的事。我想，有一个很棒的例子是多芬的"自信美人"活动。

在这个庞大的产业里，每年会砸下数十亿美元让大家看起来更耀眼、更漂亮——漂亮到超乎现实。而多芬则挑战这些始作俑者，并走到幕后告诉大家什么叫做真正的美。这是个大胆之举，有人会说这是个冒险之举，但是事实上消费者反响非常好，这证明了消费者想与品牌有更真实的关系。

Notes & Vocabulary

21. **tentacle** [ˈtɛntɪkl]
    n. 触须；触角；影响

22. **bombard** [bɑmˈbɑrd]
    v. 轰炸；投以大量信息
    Advertising messages bombard us throughout the day.

23. **submission** [sʌbˈmɪʃən]
    n. 屈服；顺从

24. **instigate** [ˈɪnstəˌget]
    v. （使）正式开始；（使）发生
    Julia always instigates arguments with her boyfriend.

25. **curator** [ˈkjʊrˌetə]
    n. 馆长；策划人；负责人

26. **transparent** [trænsˈpɛrənt]
    adj. 坦诚的；透明的
    The politician promised transparent government if elected.

27. **category** [ˈkætəˌgɔrɪ]
    n. 种类；分类；类别

28. **glamorous** [ˈglæmərəs]
    adj. 耀眼的；光彩夺目的
    The charity event attracted many glamorous celebrities.

29. **unrealistically** [ˌʌnˌriəˈlɪstɪkəlɪ]
    adv. 不实际地

30. **call sb. out** 对某人挑战；对决
    The editorial called out the mayor for breaking a campaign promise.

31. **in droves** 成群
    When salaries were cut, employees quit their jobs in droves.

32. **authentic** [ɔˈθɛntɪk]
    adj. 真正的；真实的
    The restaurant specializes in authentic Italian cuisine.

A great example of a brand understanding its own body language is Puma. And what I mean by body language of a brand is how it actually operates and exists in the real world, not just in [the] advertising world—how its values are pushed out there in the community;[33] what it does to contribute to a community; how it treats its employees; its philosophy on the environment and social issues.

I think a great example of something you've done recently, you've really looked at the packaging. I think that's a great story.

ANTONIO BERTONE, GLOBAL CMO, PUMA

Advertising is one piece of the conversation with a consumer and for us it's like how … besides attracting somebody by the products that we design and the quality that they're made [with], you know, how else do we romance[34] that relationship in order to continue that relationship forward. And packaging for me was a bit of a stickler[35] for a while because, you know, I think the global mindset[36] is trying to figure out how to be less wasteful or less harmful. We worked together with a design firm called Fuseproject and Yves Behar, and it took us just about two-and-a-half years to basically reinvent the shoebox.

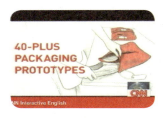

美容品牌多以美女为代言人，多芬反其道而行之，揭露广告幕后化妆修图的真相，并在各国发起 Real Beauty 活动，让女性不论身材年龄都要充满自信，接纳自己最真实的美。

01-F.MP3 / 01-S.MP3 ▌ *Modern Mad Man*

品牌了解其身体语言的一个绝佳案例是Puma。我所说的"品牌的身体语言"是指它如何在真实世界中实际运作及存在，而非只是在广告世界中，它的价值观如何在社群中推广，它对社群的贡献，它如何对待其员工，它对环境和社会议题的理念。

我想你们最近做的就是个很好的例子，你们真的查看了包装。我觉得那是个很棒的故事。

Puma 全球营销总监 安东尼奥·伯顿

广告是和消费者对话的一种方式，对我们来说它就像如何……除了用我们的产品设计和制作质量来吸引人，还要考虑如何美化与消费者的关系，好让这段关系延续下去。包装的部分已经让我烦恼了好一阵子了，因为我想全球的思维模式倾向于找出较不浪费或较无害的方法。我们和 Fuseproject 这家设计工作室合作，设计师是伊夫·巴哈。我们花了大约两年半的时间才重新设计出鞋盒。

Puma 的 Project Pink 赞助乳腺癌防治公益团体的粉红色足球运动系列。网友每次点击活动广告参与 twitter 投票，Puma 就捐出一美元。

内华达州保险产业与政府保险部合作推出的网站，给民众提供咨询并倡导保险安全。广告中用鳄鱼、豺狼影射个别恶劣的保险员冷血凶狠、嗜财如命，提醒民众谨慎选择。

图片提供：Unilever

Puma 长期赞助非洲足球队。他们特地找来纽约当红艺术家 Kehinde Wiley 为打入世界杯的球队画像并举办个展，同时用相关商品布置会场。

The Hands of Time

Generations of Skilled[1] Watchmakers Keep Piaget Ticking[2]

图片提供：PIAGET

MONITA RAJPAL, CNN ANCHOR

If you're a craftsman working for a luxury brand, the skills you have are in demand.[3] For watchmaker Piaget, those skills are not only nurtured,[4] they're protected.

The serenity of a winter's day. The site—just a 90-minute drive from the center of Geneva. This is the tiny village of La Côte-aux-Fées, population approximately 400. Yet here, nestled[5] inside the walls of this unassuming[6] building, are people creating what some consider masterpieces—Piaget watches. Only 20,000 are made a year and they range[7] anywhere from $5,000 upwards to more than a million.

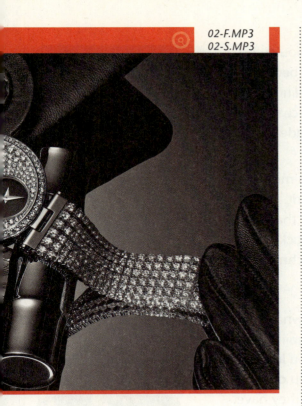

02-F.MP3
02-S.MP3

CNN 主播 莫妮塔·拉吉波

如果你是任职于某个奢侈品牌的工匠，那么你的技艺就相当抢手。对于伯爵表这家手表制造商而言，这种技艺不仅需要培养，更必须保护。

宁静的冬日。这里距离日内瓦市中心开车只要 90 分钟。这是一座叫做仙女坡的小村庄，居住着约 400 人。然而，在这栋不起眼的建筑里的人却制作着被一些人视为极品的伯爵表。伯爵表每年只生产 20 000 只，价格从 5000 美元起，最高可达 100 万美元以上。

❷ 探究百万名表的工艺价值

Notes & Vocabulary

1. **skilled** [skɪld] *adj.* 技术熟练的
   The town is known for its skilled crafts workers.

2. **tick** [tɪk]
   v. 钟表滴答运转；像机器般稳定运作
   Vanessa studies successful companies to learn what makes them tick.

3. **in demand** 供不应求
   Gold is in demand whenever the economy is suffering.

4. **nurture** [ˈnɜtʃə] *v.* 培养；扶持
   The parents nurtured their son's creative side in hopes that he would become an artist.

5. **nestle** [ˈnɛsl]
   v. 安顿；坐落于（隐蔽处）
   Many residents nestled in their homes during the cold winter months.

6. **unassuming** [ˌʌnəˈsumɪŋ]
   adj. 朴实的；不起眼的
   Paula wore an unassuming business outfit to the meeting.

7. **range** [rendʒ]
   v. 包括；（在范围内）变动；变化
   Prices for the model range from US$30,000 up to US$50,000 depending on what extras you get with it.

行业之道 | 品牌哲学 | 财经内幕 | 商海拾趣 | 环球生活

Some may wonder why a timepiece would cost that much. Well, Piaget would say it's because of this—the painstaking[8] work of assembling hundreds of miniscule[9] pieces by hand, each piece made specifically for that one model and made in-house[10] in Switzerland.

The heart of a watch may take up to a month to assemble, and that's just the movement,[11] which is the part we don't always see, the part that makes the watch do what it's meant to do—tick. And that job is down to[12] one person—the watchmaker.

PHILIPPE LEOPOLD-METZGER, CEO, PIAGET

I think they're the key. They are both what made the past and they are the one[s] that are going to make the future. I think, you know, when you look at them working and you look in their eyes, you can see the passion[13] and really the involvement[14] they have.

MONITA RAJPAL, CNN ANCHOR

This is the original facility[15] set up[16] by George Piaget in 1874. It also served[17] as the family home. Then seven decades later, this new facility was built. It's perhaps no surprise that Piaget and other watch brands have their facilities in this region of Switzerland. When you're here, you can't help but feel the stillness[18] and quiet, elements that are essential to the intricacies[19] of watchmaking and, some say, characteristics that are essential to being a good watchmaker.

有些人也许想知道一只钟表为什么会卖这么贵。伯爵会告诉你，那是因为伯爵表内数以百计的微小零件都是由手工辛苦组装成的，而且每个零件都是特别为某一表款所设计，并在瑞士由伯爵公司自行制造的。

一只表的核心部分就可能需要花上一个月的时间组装，而且这还只是我们通常看不到的机芯而已，就是这个部分让表做它该做的事——滴答运转。组装这个部分只由一个人负责——钟表匠。

伯爵公司首席执行官 菲力普·里欧帕麦赞格

我认为他们是关键人物。他们造就了过去，也将开创未来。当你看着他们工作的样子，注视着他们的眼睛时，即可看见他们的热情，以及他们对工作的投入。

CNN 主播 莫妮塔·拉吉波

这是乔治·皮亚杰在 1874 年最初选定的厂房，也是他们家族的宅邸。70 年后，又建造了这座新厂房。伯爵表和其他钟表品牌都设厂在瑞士的这个区域也许没什么好奇怪的。你一旦来到这里，自然会感受到周遭的平和宁静，而这正是钟表制作这类细致做工所不可或缺的要素，有些人更说这是杰出钟表匠的必备特质。

Notes & Vocabulary

8. **painstaking** [ˈpenˌstekɪŋ]
   adj. 辛苦的；费神的；耗费心力的
   The project will require painstaking research.

9. **miniscule** [ˈmɪnəsˌkjul]
   adj. 非常小的
   Alex cleaned the miniscule grains of sand from inside his camera.

10. **in-house** [ˈɪnˌhaus]
    adv. （在公司）内部进行地

11. **movement** [ˈmuvmənt]
    n. 钟表的机芯

12. **be down to sb.**
    由某人负责；缩减到
    The hiring for the open position is down to three final candidates.

13. **passion** [ˈpæʃən]
    n. 强烈情感；（对某活动的）热衷

14. **involvement** [ɪnˈvɑlvmənt]
    n. 投入；沉迷

15. **facility** [fəˈsɪlətɪ]
    n. 设施；（供特定用途的）场所

16. **set up** 建立；创立
    Andrew set up a clothing factory in Manila last year.

17. **serve** [sɜv]
    v. 可用作；可当……使用
    The cave served as a shelter for the survivors of the plane crash.

18. **stillness** [ˈstɪlnəs] *n.* 安静；宁静

19. **intricacy** [ˈɪntrəkəsɪ]
    n. 错综复杂的事物或细节

JACQUES-ANDRES PIAGET, WATCHMAKER

You have to be someone calm, someone who's very careful and well-trained.

MONITA RAJPAL, CNN ANCHOR

The skills take years to perfect, and for Jacques-Andres Piaget, a descendant[20] of the brand's founder, George Piaget, it's a craft he has been perfecting for almost half a century.

JACQUES-ANDRES PIAGET, WATCHMAKER

I always wanted to be a watchmaker. My father was a watchmaker. My grandfather was a watchmaker. My great grandfather was a watchmaker. And I wanted to continue the tradition.

MONITA RAJPAL, CNN ANCHOR

But not everyone has tradition behind them. While the region boasts[21] many from watchmaking families, this is a profession that at one point saw a decline[22] with many young people opting[23] for other industries. This prompted[24] the Swiss government to step in[25] and invest in their centuries-old heritage[26] of watchmaking. Schools were funded and brands encouraged to partner with them with [in] apprenticeship[27] programs.

How important is it for Piaget to nurture skills for watchmakers and to maintain the skills that they have?

钟表匠 雅克安德烈斯·皮亚杰

你必须是个冷静的人,很细心且训练有素。

CNN 主播 莫妮塔·拉吉波

制表的技艺需要花上许多年才能臻于纯熟。身为伯爵表创始人乔治·皮亚杰的后代,雅克安德烈斯·皮亚杰在这项技艺上精益求精已达半个世纪之久。

钟表匠 雅克安德烈斯·皮亚杰

我一直想当钟表匠。我的父亲是钟表匠,我的祖父是钟表匠,我的曾祖父也是钟表匠。我想要延续这种传统。

CNN 主播 莫妮塔·拉吉波

不过,不是每个人背后都有一段传统。这个地区虽然有许多人都出身钟表匠世家,这项职业却曾一度因为许多年轻人选择其他行业而转趋没落。这促使瑞士政府出手相助,为该国长达数百年的钟表制作传统投资。政府资助建校,并鼓励各钟表品牌与学校合作推行学徒项目。

对伯爵表而言,培养钟表匠的技艺以及维持他们的技艺水平有多重要?

20. **descendant** [dɪˈsɛndənt]
    n. 后裔;后代

21. **boast** [bost]
    v. 以有……而自豪;拥有
    Napa and Sonoma counties in California boast many fine wineries.

22. **decline** [dɪˈklaɪn] *n.* 衰退;减少

23. **opt** [ɑpt] *v.* 选择
    Brian opted to forego college and begin working for his father's business.

24. **prompt** [prɑmpt] *v.* 促使;导致
    Concern over the environment prompted many drivers to purchase hybrid vehicles.

25. **step in** 伸出援手;干预
    The EU stepped in to help several countries with sagging economies.

26. **heritage** [ˈhɛrətɪdʒ]
    n.(历史、文化等)遗产

27. **apprenticeship** [əˈprɛntəsˌʃɪp]
    n. 学徒工作;学徒制

行业之道 | 品牌哲学 | 财经内幕 | 商海拾趣 | 环球生活

YVES BORNAND, HUMAN RESOURCES MANAGER, PIAGET
It is very important indeed, due to the fact that each year we have more technological products, movements, so it is important that we stick to our knowledge and we improve it also.

MONITA RAJPAL, CNN ANCHOR
And when there is an unstable economy, those skills acquired[28] become valuable assets, almost assuring job security. Last year when Piaget had to reduce production as a response to the recession,[29] it made sure that their skilled craftsmen were not touched.[30]

PHILIPPE LEOPOLD-METZGER, CEO, PIAGET
The most important thing for us was to manage production, but to make sure that we would lose none of the expertise,[31] and those people are expensive. Watchmakers today and skilled workers are making very good money. And yes, they are protected because they are our future.

伯爵公司人力资源经理 依维斯·博南德

这点确实非常重要。我们每年都会推出更多的科技产品，例如机芯。所以保持我们的知识并加以精进真的很重要。

CNN 主播 莫妮塔·拉吉波

经济形势一旦不稳定，这种不容易学的技艺就成了珍贵的资产，几乎是工作的保障。去年，伯爵表虽然为了适应经济衰退而不得不减产，却仍要确保这些技术高超的工匠不会受到影响。

伯爵公司首席执行官 菲力普·里欧帕麦赞格

对我们而言，最重要的事情就是管理生产，并确保不因此丧失专业性。这些人力可是非常昂贵的。当今的钟表匠与技术劳工可以赚取可观的收入。没错，他们之所以受到保护，就是因为他们是我们的未来。

Notes & Vocabulary

28. **acquire** [əˋkwaɪr] *v.* 获得；学到
Bill's son acquired some bad habits in kindergarten.

29. **recession** [rɪˋsɛʃən]
n. 经济衰退

30. **touch** [tʌtʃ] *v.* 影响；触及
Melody didn't touch her savings account for several years and now she has enough money to retire.

31. **expertise** [ˌɛkspɝˋtiz]
n. 专门技能

行业之道

品牌哲学

财经内幕

商海拾趣

环球生活

E-Reader Revolution[1]

More Book Lovers Forsake[2] Paper as the Electronic Medium[3] Takes Off

图片提供 :Kindle

ZANE VERJEE, CNN ANCHOR

Electronic readers have seen a big jump in sales this year. They've been around for a while now, but there's been a sudden boost.[4] Megan Hughes reads between the lines.

MEGAN HUGHES, CNN CORRESPONDENT

When you hit[5] the beach this summer, what kind of book will you bring: old-fashioned paperback[6] or

03-F.MP3
03-S.MP3

Notes & Vocabulary

标题扫描

take off 大受欢迎；起飞

take off 常见用法是指飞机或事业"起飞"，此处则是指商品突然大受欢迎、销量大增，或观念迅速流行。

- The popularity of the novel **took off** after Oprah included it in her book club.
  这部小说被欧普拉列入读书会清单后就突然大受欢迎。

- The plane **took off** despite the poor weather.
  尽管天气不佳，飞机还是起飞了。

read between the lines
明白言外之意

字面上是"阅读字里行间"的意思，表示试图参透其中的意义，即"明白言外之意"。

- Bonnie **read between the lines** of John's message to understand that he was breaking up with her.
  邦妮细读约翰留下的便条的含意，明白他要与她分手。

1. **revolution** [ˌrɛvəˈluʃən]
   n. 革命；大变革

2. **forsake** [fəˈsek]
   v. 摒弃；离开（喜爱的事物）
   Many viewers forsook the television series when the plot took a strange turn.

3. **medium** [ˈmidiəm]
   n. （传播信息的）媒介

4. **boost** [bust] *n.* 增长；提高

5. **hit** [hɪt] *v.* 到达（某地）
   Mike hit the mall after school.

6. **paperback** [ˈpepɚˌbæk]
   n. 平装书；简装书

CNN 主播 洁茵·维尔吉

电子书在今年销量大增，电子书上市已有一段时间，但是直到最近才大放异彩。梅根·休斯一窥其中端倪。

CNN 特派员 梅根·休斯

今年夏天到海滩玩，你会带哪种书呢？老式

行业之道

品牌哲学

财经内幕

商海拾趣

环球生活

high-tech e-reader? While some say they prefer not to hop[7] on the e-train…

UNIDENTIFIED FEMALE

There's something I like about holding a book in my hands and looking at the cover and turning the pages.

MEGAN HUGHES, CNN CORRESPONDENT

… others have grown to love the edge[8] the devices[9] have to offer.

UNIDENTIFIED MALE

Not needing to ship around dead tree bark.[10]

MEGAN HUGHES, CNN CORRESPONDENT

Or the fact that you can buy new books without hitting a bookstore.

UNIDENTIFIED MALE

Or you can load it from the airplane or the airport or while you're on a cruise ship.[11]

MEGAN HUGHES, CNN CORRESPONDENT

And now with lower prices, more people can get on board before getting away. Sony, Barnes and Noble and Amazon have shaved the price off[12] their e-readers to under 200 bucks.

Barnes and Noble execs[13] say part of the reason for the price cut was a big summer reading push, but another reason could be a pricier[14] and higher-tech competitor with the introduction of the iPad.

的平装书还是高科技的电子书?虽然有些人表示他们不想跳上电子化的列车。

不知名女子

我喜欢手中拿着书本的感觉,能看到封面而且能够翻页。

CNN 特派员 梅根·休斯

其他人却逐渐爱上了这些电子装置的优点。

不知名男士

不必再运载死亡的树皮。

CNN 特派员 梅根·休斯

或者其实你不必进书店就可以买到新书。

不知名男士

你可以在飞机上或是机场,甚至是在搭乘游艇时下载书籍。

CNN 特派员 梅根·休斯

现在,更多人可以在度假前就能以更低的价格赶上这股热潮。索尼、邦诺和亚马逊都已将电子书的价格砍到 200 美元以下了。

邦诺的高层主管表示,降价的部分原因是赶夏日的读书热潮,但另外一个原因可能是因为即将上市的价格更高的高科技竞争者——iPad。

7. **hop** [hɑp]
   v. 登上(飞机、汽车、火车等)
   Many people hopped on the team's bandwagon when they started winning games.

8. **edge** [ɛdʒ] *n.* 优势

9. **device** [dəˋvaɪs] *n.* 装置;设备

10. **bark** [bɑrk] *n.* 树皮

11. **cruise ship** [krus] [ʃɪp]
    游轮;游艇

12. **shave off**(微量地)减少;缩小
    Ben shaved off 10 minutes from his commute by taking a bus.

13. **exec** [ɪgˋzɛk]
    n. 经理;管理人员(= executive)

14. **pricey** [ˋpraɪsɪ] *adj.* 昂贵的
    Phil eats at pricey restaurants when he uses the company's expense account.

行业之道 | 品牌哲学 | 财经内幕 | 商海拾趣 | 环球生活

UNIDENTIFIED MALE

You just touch the corner and it'll flip to the next page.

MEGAN HUGHES, CNN CORRESPONDENT

iPads boast[15] color touch screens and have a lot more uses but carry a starting price tag of 500 bucks. Compare that to a $15 paperback bestseller.[16]

Market analyst[17] Michael Norris says that's why less than 10 percent of the population bought an e-book last year. There are still some bonuses[18] to books at the beach.

电子书　图解单词

screen 屏幕

previous page 上一页

next page 下一页

keyboard 键盘

home 首页

next page 下一页

menu 目录

back 返回

memory card slot 记忆卡槽

touch screen 触控式屏幕

reset 重新设定

USB port USB 接头

volume 音量调整

power plug 电源插槽

headphone jack 耳机插槽

图片提供：Marit & Toomas Hinnosaar、Amazon Kindle、robertnelson

不知名男士

你只要轻轻按一下角落，它就会翻到下一页。

CNN 特派员 梅根·休斯

iPad 自夸拥有彩色的触控屏幕和许多其他功能，但是它的定价却要 500 美元起。和 15 美元的平装畅销书比比吧。

市场分析师麦克·诺里斯表示这就是为什么去年只有不到 10% 的人买了电子书。看来带本纸质书去海滩还是多数人的选择。

15. **boast** [bost]

    v. 自夸；以拥有……自豪

    The hotel room boasts a large flat-screen television.

16. **bestseller** [ˋbɛstˏsɛləˋ]

    n. 畅销书

17. **analyst** [ˋænəlɪst]

    n. 分析师

18. **bonus** [ˋbonəs]

    n. 意外收获；津贴

行业之道 | 品牌哲学 | 财经内幕 | 商海拾趣 | 环球生活

电子书大评比

型 号	Amazon Kindle 3 (3G+Wi-Fi)	Barnes & Noble Nook (3G + Wi-Fi)
上市日期	2010/7/28	2009/11/30
产品尺寸	7.5 x 4.8 x 0.36 英寸（注）	7.7 x 4.9 x 0.5 英寸
屏幕大小	7.5 x 4.8 x 0.36 英寸	6 寸黑白屏幕
重 量	优 250 g	343g
容 量	内存 4 GB	内存 2 GB
上市定价	优 189 美元	259 美元
目前售价	189 美元	199 美元 (2010/6)
特 色	• 另有 Wi-Fi 版，售价 139 美元 • 支持更多字体	• 另有 3.5 寸彩色屏幕 • 另有 Wi-Fi 版，售价 149 美元

图片提供：Marit & Toomas Hinnosaar、Barnes & Noble Nook、Amazon Kindle、Apple Inc.

注：1 英寸 =2.54 厘米

Sony **PRS-600**	Apple 平板电脑 **iPad**
2009/8	2010/4/3
6.9 x 4.8 x 0.4 英寸	9.56 x 7.47 x 0.53 英寸
6 寸三色触控屏幕	优 9.7 寸彩色触控屏幕
286 g	680 g
内存 512/380 MB	优 内存 16/32/64 GB
249.99 美元	499 美元起
优 169.99 美元	499 美元起
• 可搜索正文 • 内置字典、可调整字体大小 • 外壳有三色可选	• 具 Wi-Fi 功能 • 使用电子书软件 iBook • 另有 3G 版

行业之道

品牌哲学

财经内幕

商海拾趣

环球生活

Home Shopping Chic[1]

Hot Designers and Devoted[2] Customers Flock[3] to Cable TV's Virtual[4] Malls

COLLEEN MCEDWARDS, CNN ANCHOR

Well for years, buying things on TV shopping channels usually meant buying, you know, cheap or tacky[5] products that were sold by overly excited pitchmen,[6] but no more. The U.S. channel QVC has attracted top designers to its airwaves,[7] selling some 166 million products worldwide last year. Alina Cho takes a look at QVC's new image.

ALINA CHO, CNN CORRESPONDENT

It was a little shaky[8] in the early days.

04-F.MP3
04-S.MP3

CNN 主播 柯琳·麦克艾德华

多年来，在电视购物频道上购物，买到的不是廉价货就是俗不可耐的商品，而且推销的主持人总是一副兴奋过度的模样。不过，这种情况已经改变了。美国电视频道 QVC 引进了顶尖设计师，去年卖出了 1.66 亿件商品。周艾琳要带我们探究 QVC 的新形象。

CNN 特派员 周艾琳

QVC 初期不是很稳定。

Notes & Vocabulary

1. **chic** [ʃɪk] *n.* 时髦；高尚

2. **devoted** [dɪˋvotəd]
   adj. 忠诚的；全心全意的
   The singer has many devoted fans.

3. **flock** [flɑk] *v.* 聚集；蜂拥
   Many shoppers in the U.S. flock to shopping malls the day after the Thanksgiving holiday.

4. **virtual** [ˋvɝtʃuəl] *adj.* 虚拟的
   The Web site is described as an online virtual department store.

5. **tacky** [ˋtækɪ] *adj.* 低劣的；俗气的
   Jim wore a tacky shirt to the dress-up party.

6. **pitchman** [ˋpɪtʃmən]
   n. 商品宣传者

7. **airwave** [ˋɛrˌwev]
   n. 电视、广播的频道

8. **shaky** [ˋʃekɪ]
   adj. 不稳固的；不牢靠的
   The meeting got off to a shaky start when Dan realized he had forgotten his notes.

QVC HOST
Everybody wants this ladder. I live in an apartment with vaulted[9] ceilings. Uh-oh.

ALINA CHO, CNN CORRESPONDENT
That was then.

HARRY SLATKIN, QVC DESIGNER
They're not in Kansas anymore as they would have said in *The Wizard of Oz*. They've arrived.

ALINA CHO, CNN CORRESPONDENT
This is now. Founded in 1986, QVC, the 24-hour TV network for at-home shoppers, is now an **$8 billion** business. But here's the real news: Among the big-name designer set, QVC is suddenly cool.

ISAAC MIZRAHI, QVC DESIGNER
It's mesmerizing,[10] but on top of that,[11] now it really looks great.

ALINA CHO, CNN CORRESPONDENT
QVC is so selective, it's reported thousands apply for just a few spots.[12] Like Isaac Mizrahi, Diane von Fürstenberg and Vivienne Tam. Dennis Basso, furrier[13] to the stars, is on Madison Avenue and on QVC selling faux[14] fur amounting to[15] tens of millions in sales, and it's not just designers.

KIM KARDASHIAN, CELEBUTANTE, QVC DESIGNER
You just have to feel how stretchy this is.

QVC 节目主持人

每个人都想要一把这种梯子。我住的公寓就有拱形天花板。喔。

CNN 特派员　周艾琳

那段时期已经过去了。

QVC 设计师　哈利·史拉特金

就像《绿野仙踪》里面说的，他们已经不在堪萨斯了，环境已经变了。他们脱胎换骨了。

CNN 特派员　周艾琳

这是现在的模样。QVC 创立于 1986 年，是 24 小时无休、专为居家消费者服务的电视台，目前营业额已达 80 亿美元。不过，真正令人惊讶的是，对于知名设计师设计的商品而言，QVC 突然成了极具魅力的销售渠道。

QVC 设计师　艾萨克·麦兹拉西

这个电视台确实令人着迷。更重要的是，现在他们的节目看起来也很棒。

CNN 特派员　周艾琳

QVC 的筛选标准非常严格，据说有好几千名设计师争着抢那少数几个时段，例如艾萨克·麦兹拉西、戴安·范·富丝坦堡与谭燕玉。明星的皮草供货商丹尼斯·巴索在麦迪逊大道和 QVC 上销售人造皮草，销售额高达好几千万。而且，争着上 QVC 的还不只是设计师而已。

QVC 设计师及交际花　金·卡黛珊

你一定要感受一下这个弹性有多好。

Notes & Vocabulary

not in Kansas anymore
物换星移

这是出自《绿野仙踪》的经典台词 "Toto, I've a feeling we're not in Kansas anymore."，后来 not in Kansas anymore 被延伸用来形容"环境已改变、物换星移"，因此得要试着适应。

When the founders of the small start-up received their first large venture capital investment, they knew they weren't in Kansas anymore.
这家创业小公司的创办人们获得第一笔巨额投资时，他们知道情况已不可同日而语了。

9. **vaulted** [ˈvɔltɪd]
adj. 拱形的；有拱顶的
Many older churches have vaulted ceilings.

10. **mesmerize** [ˈmɛsməˌraɪz]
v. 迷住；吸引
The juggler mesmerized his young audience.

11. **on top of that** 最重要的是
The shop sells quality products and on top of that, their prices can't be beat.

12. **spot** [spɑt]
n. (电视、广播中)定期小节目；(节目间的)广告插播

13. **furrier** [ˈfɜrɪə]
n. 毛皮加工者；毛皮商

14. **faux** [fo] *adj.* 【法】假的；人造
The coat was made of faux leather.

15. **amount to** 总计；共计
Bonnie felt her manager's criticism of her work amounted to a personal attack.

行业之道　品牌哲学　财经内幕　商海拾趣　环球生活

ALINA CHO, CNN CORRESPONDENT

Even the Kardashian sisters are getting into the game, but in order to stay, you have to sell.

Pressure's on. When you're on, it's like sell, sell, sell.

KIM KARDASHIAN, CELEBUTANTE, QVC DESIGNER

Yeah, you have to sell, so we try and just give as much information as we know about the products and why we love them, why we created it, what the fit's like, what the cut's like and it helps for them to see it on us.

ALINA CHO, CNN CORRESPONDENT

It's all part of the game.

FERN MALLIS, STYLE EXPERT

They psych into the consumers in a way that nobody does. They know, they know. They know how to move goods. It's a fascinating thing to watch.

ALINA CHO, CNN CORRESPONDENT

Show hosts caress[16] handbags, and what about candles? How do you sell products you can't smell?

HARRY SLATKIN, QVC DESIGNER

Caramel,[17] nutmeg.[18]

ALINA CHO, CNN CORRESPONDENT

There are tricks to selling.

CNN 特派员 周艾琳

连卡黛珊姐妹花都加入了这场游戏。不过，若想留下来，就必须交出业绩。

压力很大。你一旦上场，就得不断地卖，不断地卖。

QVC 设计师及交际花 金·卡黛珊

是啊，你一定要卖出成绩，所以我们对产品所知的一切都会尽量说出来，并且说明我们为什么喜欢这款产品，为什么会制作这款产品，版型怎么样，剪裁怎么样。而且，我们穿在身上展示，消费者就能够看出衣服的特色。

CNN 特派员 周艾琳

他们就是这样做的。

造型专家 冯恩·美力斯

他们比谁都了解（注）消费者。他们就是知道。他们懂得怎么卖东西，看他们推销商品确实很有趣。

CNN 特派员 周艾琳

节目主持人可以抚摸手提包，但蜡烛怎么办？你要怎么给观众推销闻不到气味的商品？

QVC 设计师 哈利·史拉特金

焦糖，肉豆蔻。

CNN 特派员 周艾琳

推销是有诀窍的。

注：psych 在此意同 figure out 或 understand，通常写作 psych out。

Notes & Vocabulary

part of the game
就是如此；理所当然

字面上是 "游戏的一部分" 的意思，用来说明事情就是如此，正如游戏规则一般。

- In business and sports, psyching out the competition is part of the game.
  在商业与运动领域中，恫吓对手是理所当然的。

16. **caress** [kə`rɛs] *v.* 抚摸；爱抚
    Bonnie caressed her sick daughter's cheek to comfort her.

17. **caramel** [`kærəməl]
    n. 焦糖

18. **nutmeg** [`nʌtˌmɛg]
    n. 肉豆蔻

行业之道

品牌哲学

财经内幕

商海拾趣

环球生活

HARRY SLATKIN, QVC DESIGNER
They'll tell me when I'm saying something to go back and say it because the customer reacts to it.

ALINA CHO, CNN CORRESPONDENT
Then there's the interaction with designers that customers don't get in a store. Like a product? Don't like it? Call in.

QVC HOST
Are you getting our "today's special value"?

FEMALE CUSTOMER
Oh, yes, in the amethyst.[19]

ALINA CHO, CNN CORRESPONDENT
They get to talk to you on the phone.

ISAAC MIZRAHI, QVC DESIGNER
That's my favorite part. That is my favorite part.

ALINA CHO, CNN CORRESPONDENT
And that connection breeds[20] loyalty; 95 percent of QVC's revenue comes from repeat customers.

MIKE GEORGE, PRESIDENT AND CEO, QVC
And our numbers tell us that if you make two or three purchases on QVC, you will be a customer for life.

QVC 设计师 哈利·史拉特金

有时候他们会要求我重复说某句话，因为顾客会被那句话调动起来。

CNN 特派员 周艾琳

此外，消费者在 QVC 上还可以和设计师互动，这是在店里得不到的体验。喜欢某件商品吗？不喜欢？打电话进去表达意见吧。

QVC 节目主持人

你要订购我们的"本日特价商品"吗？

女性顾客

是的，紫色的那件。

CNN 特派员 周艾琳

他们可以通过电话和你对话。

QVC 设计师 艾萨克·麦兹拉西

那是我最喜欢的部分，那是我最喜欢的部分。

CNN 特派员 周艾琳

这样的交流可培养客户的忠诚度。QVC 的营业额当中，有 95% 都来自老顾客。

QVC 总裁兼首席执行官 迈克·乔治

我们从统计数据中发现，你如果在 QVC 频道上买过两三次东西，就会成为我们的终生顾客。

Notes & Vocabulary

19. **amethyst** [ˈæməθəst]
n. 紫水晶；紫色

20. **breed** [brid] *v.* 培育；养成
The government's lack of transparency breeds public distrust.

ALINA CHO, CNN CORRESPONDENT

New designer Coralie Charriol's family is in the luxury jewelry business, but when she started her own brand, she wanted to go affordable[21] selling handbags on QVC. Her task on this night? Sell 800 in 15 minutes.

CORALIE CHARRIOL PAUL, QVC DESIGNER

So, fewer than 200 bags remaining. The plum[22] is completely sold out.

And you hear, "This color is not available anymore." You're like "Yes! Somebody likes what I'm doing!"

CNN 特派员 周艾琳

新设计师可拉莉·查里欧的家族从事名贵珠宝行业，但她创立自己的品牌时，却希望走平价路线，于是到 QVC 频道上推销手提包。她今晚的工作是什么呢？15 分钟内卖出 800 个包包。

QVC 设计师 可拉莉·查里欧·保罗

接下来只剩下不到 200 个包包了。紫红色的已经全部卖完了。

你会听到："这个颜色已经卖完了。"这时候你就会觉得："太好了！观众喜欢我的表现！"

21. **affordable** [əˈfɔrdəbl]
adj. 负担得起的
The affordable housing development is intended for first-time buyers.

22. **plum** [plʌm] *n.* 梅子；紫红色

行业之道 品牌哲学 财经内幕 商海拾趣 环球生活

行业之道 ❺ 视频网站"征战"正酣

Live and Uncensored[1]

Video Sites Challenge YouTube's Dominance[2] of the Online Frontier

图片提供：Reuters

CNN ANCHOR

A ruthless[3] new battle is raging[4] online.

CNN ANCHOR

That's right, a rash of[5] start-up Web sites are pursuing[6] a slice of the action triggered[7] by the YouTube phenomenon and they're doing whatever it takes to win users.

05-F.MP3
05-S.MP3

CNN 女主播

网络上正掀起一场无情的新战争。

CNN 男主播

没错，YouTube 风潮让许多新成立的网站争相效仿，这些网站正在无所不用其极地争取用户。

Notes & Vocabulary

a slice of the action 插一脚

名词 slice 是指"薄片；切片"，action 在这里是指某事带来的"作用"。a slice of the action 在文中表示许多新兴的网站都想"分一杯羹、沾一点好处"。

· Many construction companies wanted a slice of the action in the land deal.
许多建筑公司都想在那项土地项目中插一脚。

同义词

▶ a piece of the action
  = a slice of the pie / cake
  = slice of the profits

1. **uncensored** [ʌn`sɛnsəd]
   adj. 无约束的；未经审查的
   The cable channel screened an uncensored version of the movie.

2. **dominance** [`dɑmənəns]
   n. 统治（地位）

3. **ruthless** [`ruθlɪs]
   adj. 无情的；残忍的
   The CEO was known to be a ruthless businessman.

4. **rage** [redʒ] *v.* 盛行；激烈进行
   Outside, the storm raged.

5. **a rash of** 大量的……
   There was a rash of burglaries in the neighborhood.

6. **pursue** [pə`su] *v.* 追求
   The government pursued a new strategy to combat poverty.

7. **trigger** [`trɪgə] *v.* 引发；引起
   Certain forms of illness can be triggered by food allergies.

行业之道

品牌哲学

财经内幕

商海拾趣

环球生活

CNN ANCHOR

Alphonso Van Marsh logs on to the wild frontier that is cyberspace.[8]

ALPHONSO VAN MARSH, CNN CORRESPONDENT

These are the images of Saddam Hussein as shown on most television networks. But people are watching the graphic[9] video unedited on the Internet. And it's not just obscure[10] sites, but big brand names like Google Video and YouTube. And that's surprising some technology analysts, given Google recently paid hundreds of millions of dollars to buy the YouTube brand.

STEVE MULLINS, EDITOR, INFORMA TELECOMS AND MEDIA

When you pay 1.65 billion, you want to protect your property and you don't want that property demeaned[11] by being associated with—what should we call it?—unsavory[12] material such as the Saddam Hussein execution video.

CNN 女主播

阿方索·范马许前往网络这个蛮荒世界一窥究竟。

CNN 特派员 阿方索·范马许

这些是在大部分电视台中播放的萨达姆画面。但大家却在因特网上观赏这段未经剪辑、原始呈现的影片。播放这些影片的不只是名不见经传的网站，还包括像 Google Video 和 YouTube 这类大型的知名网站。一些科技分析师对此感到十分惊讶，因为 Google 不久前才花了数十亿美元买下 YouTube 这个品牌（注 1）。

资讯电信媒体公司编辑 史提夫·穆林

如果你花了 16.5 亿美元，你当然想保护你的资产，而且会不希望那份资产因为让人反感的内容而贬损了价值，比如像萨达姆遭到处决的影片。

注 1：Google 在 2006 年 10 月 9 日宣布，以 16.5 亿美元股票并购视频分享网站 YouTube，这是 Google 有史以来金额最高的并购案。并购之后，YouTube 仍将独立运作，保留其品牌与社群运作。

Notes & Vocabulary

be associated with
与……有关；被牵连到

associate 是指"联想；联系起来"，be associated with 解释为"与……有关联；与……有瓜葛"，并非指真正涉入其中。

- Several symptoms are associated with the disease.
  这一些病症让人联想到是否与该疾病有关。

associate 不同词性的解释与用法

associate with *v.* 结交；交往
- The party members rarely associate with their political rivals.
  该党党员与其政治对手极少互动。

associate *n.* 伙伴；同事；合伙人
- Roger took several business associates to dinner.
  罗杰请了几位同事去吃晚餐。

---

8. **cyberspace** [ˈsaɪbɚˌspes]
   n. 网络空间

9. **graphic** [ˈɡræfɪk]
   adj. 写实的；血淋淋的
   The film contained graphic violence.

10. **obscure** [əbˈskjʊr]
    adj. 无名的；没名气的
    The report cited several obscure sources.

11. **demean** [dɪˈmin]
    v. 贬低……的地位
    Critics say rap music often demeans women.

12. **unsavory** [ʌnˈsevərɪ]
    adj. 名誉不好的
    An unsavory stranger was spotted in the neighborhood.

ALPHONSO VAN MARSH, CNN CORRESPONDENT

The Saddam execution video is the latest clip[13] getting millions of views in the online world of video sharing, where offerings range from the modest to the mundane.[14] People can post just about anything online. Most of the shared video sites are based in the [United] States where free speech is constitutionally[15] protected. But there's a growing number of new generation sites in other countries vying[16] to be the next YouTube—uncensored sites like Britain's Liveleak.com, also showing the Saddam video and other clips of questionable taste.

BRYAN CLICK, EDITOR, COMPUTING

We are very much in the gold rush stage, I think, for video sharing sites. And so there's a lot of Internet entrepreneurs[17] who are looking at that and thinking, well hey you know, this is a big and very rapidly growing pie and I want a slice of it. You know, I think it's one of those areas we'll see a lot more copycat[18] sites coming up over the next year or two.

CNN 特派员 阿方索·范马许

　　萨达姆遭处决的影片是最近在视频网站上点击量达数千万次的影片。而视频网站上的影片内容则是包罗万象。无论什么样的内容都能贴上网络。绝大多数共享影片的网站地址都设在言论自由受到宪法保障的美国。但有越来越多位于其他国家的新一代网站争相成为下一个 YouTube，像内容未经检查的英国网站 Liveleak.com 也在播放萨达姆的那段影片和其他品味可疑的短片。

COMPUTING 杂志编辑 布莱恩·克里克

　　我认为影片共享网站现在处于淘金热的阶段，所以有很多网络创业者看到这个现象后会想，这是个规模庞大又成长迅速的市场，我也想从中分一杯羹。我认为像这一类的领域在未来一到两年内还会出现更多靠抄袭而"上位"的网站。

Notes & Vocabulary

gold rush 淘金热

gold rush 原指 19 世纪在北美及澳大利亚等地的"淘金热潮"，rush 是"大量激增；涌现"的意思，形容淘金人一窝蜂聚集到有金矿的地区。gold rush 在此则是比喻这些影片共享网站大量出现，如当时的淘金热一般，许多人狂热地一头栽入，希望能捞一笔钱。

- The invention of the PC ushered in a technological gold rush.
  个人计算机的发明开启了科技热潮。

rush 不同词性的解释与用法

rush (to V) *v.* 急忙（去做某事）
- Megan rushed to finish cooking dinner before her guests arrived.
  梅根赶忙在客人到之前做好饭。

rush *n.* 匆忙；仓促
- William left for work in a rush.
  威廉匆忙地离开办公室。

13. clip [klɪp] *n.* 影片

14. mundane [mʌnˋden] *adj.* 世俗的
    Ben enjoys a relatively mundane life.

15. constitutionally
    [ˌkɑnstəˋtuʃənəlɪ] *adv.* 宪法上地

16. vie [vaɪ] *v.* 竞争；竞赛
    Several candidates are vying for the presidency.

17. entrepreneur [ˌɑntrəprəˋnɝ]
    n. 创业者；企业家

18. copycat [ˋkɑpɪˌkæt]
    n. 抄袭者；模仿者

行业之道 ｜ 品牌哲学 ｜ 财经内幕 ｜ 商海拾趣 ｜ 环球生活

ALPHONSO VAN MARSH, CNN CORRESPONDENT

Most video sharing sites don't charge money to post, watch or download video. They make their money from advertising. So the more controversy[19] they have to drive more Internet users to a web page, the more visibility[20] and more potential business advertisers get from consumers.

So in an age when a video sharing savvy[21] you is named *Time* magazine's "Person of the Year," it seems there's a hungry audience to support a new generation of dot-coms looking to cash in on the banal[22] and the bizarre.[23]

CNN 特派员 阿方索 · 范马许

绝大部分的视频网站不会对发布、观赏或下载影片收取费用，他们是靠广告来赚钱的。因此视频争议性越高，就越能吸引更多网络用户浏览，曝光度就越高，也就越能从观众中找到潜在的广告客户。

因此，在你熟知视频网站的这个年代，一个名为"时代杂志年度风云人物"的共享视频背后，也许正有一批新的网络公司被网友的饥渴情绪推动着，利用形形色色的影片踏上了捞金之路。

注 2：dot 是英文符号"."，而 com 则是 comercial "商业的"的缩写，用在电子邮件地址以及网址的最后。文中的 dot-com 是名词，即 dot-com company，指利用网络提供服务或产品的公司。

Notes & Vocabulary

cash in (on)

利用；（靠）……赚钱

cash in 在此是"利用……牟利；靠……赚钱"的意思，后面接介词 on。

- The quiz show winner cashed in on his newfound fame.
  益智问答节目的优胜者靠着他刚走红的名气赚钱。

其他有关 cash in 的用法

cash in one's chips

去世；一命呜呼

- After years of living the good life to excess, the aging Hollywood star finally cashed in his chips.
  过了多年奢华无度的生活后，那位上了年纪的好莱坞明星终于一命呜呼了。

19. **controversy** [ˈkɑntrəˌvɜsɪ]
    n. 争议；争论

20. **visibility** [ˌvɪzəˈbɪlətɪ]
    n. 能见度；曝光率

21. **savvy** [ˈsævɪ]
    v. 懂；知晓

22. **banal** [bəˈnɑl] adj. 平庸的
    The banal stage play was panned by critics.

23. **bizarre** [bɪˈzɑr] adj. 奇异的；怪异的
    Several people commented on Nick's bizarre behavior.

行业之道　品牌哲学　财经内幕　商海拾趣　环球生活

品牌哲学

Hamburgerology 101

McDonald's University Trains the Next Crop[1] of Big Mac Managers

图片提供：c 2010 McDonald's

ANDREW STEVENS, CNN ANCHOR

Now, to a university that's turning out[2] some of the world's top hamburger experts. You might not have heard of the ~~Ohio~~ [Illinois] campus, but you'll recognize its logo in a flash. *CNN Money* reporter Poppy Harlow gives us an exclusive look at the crash course[3] which has been producing Big Mac management professionals for more than half a century.

POPPY HARLOW, CNN MONEY

Well, from Shanghai to Brazil to Chicago, more than a quarter million people have graduated from McDonald's Hamburger University. It is McDonald's training ground for their high-potential employees, and they graduate with a degree in

❻ 从 "汉堡" 大学看麦当劳的员工训练哲学

Notes & Vocabulary

标题扫描

Hamburgerology 101
词尾 –ology 是 "学科" 的意思, 所以 **hamburgerology** 就是 "汉堡学", 一般是指麦当劳的员工训练课程, 101 则是美国大多数一年级入门课程的编号, 所以就泛指 "入门; 基础; 导读" 的意思。

in a flash
瞬间; 迅速地
flash 是 "闪光; 一闪; 闪现", 是很短暂的时间, 故 **in a flash** 就表示 "瞬间; 立即; 迅速"。

·The chef had the order prepared in a flash.
那位主厨一下子就把点的菜做好了。

同义词

= at a glance; in a glimpse

CNN 主播 安德鲁 · 史帝芬斯

　　现在, 来看一所培育世界顶尖汉堡专家的大学。你可能没听过伊利诺伊校区, 但是你马上就能认出它的商标。《CNN 钱线》记者芭比 · 哈洛带我们一探究竟, 看看这个在半个多世纪以来培育了许多汉堡管理专业人才的速成课程。

《CNN 钱线》芭比 · 哈洛

　　从上海、巴西到芝加哥, 超过 25 万人已从麦当劳汉堡大学毕业。这是用来训练高潜力员工的培训基地。他们毕业时会有汉堡学的

1. **crop** [krɑp]
   n. (同时做某事的) 一批人

2. **turn out** 训练出; 生产出
   The business school turns out some of the world's top CEOs and leaders of industry.

3. **crash course** [kræʃ] [kɔrs]
   n. 速成课程

行业之道　品牌哲学　财经内幕　商海拾趣　环球生活

hamburgerology. As you can see, we took a visit for ourselves.

McDonald's serves 60 million people a day, but here at Hamburger U, students don't learn how to flip burgers. The food is actually fake. These students are learning the management skills to make a restaurant hum[4] in a five-day course, grooming[5] them to be owners.

In the first simulation,[6] long lines, frustrated customers and flustered[7] managers, then the orders get more complicated, designed to test the limits of the operation.

FEMALE HAMBURGER UNIVERSITY INSTRUCTOR
How do you think this is impacting your customers?

FEMALE STUDENT
Everybody is getting upset. All you see is the manager running back and forth[8] and not really helping. It's more chaotic[9] than anything else.

POPPY HARLOW, CNN MONEY
So, back to class.

FEMALE HAMBURGER UNIVERSITY INSTRUCTOR
All right, my teams. Should we talk about what just happened?

MALE STUDENT
They were friendly. I just wasn't getting my food very quickly.

学位，就像你看到的。我们亲自走访一趟。

麦当劳一天为 6000 万名顾客服务，但是在汉堡大学这里，学生并不会学如何给汉堡翻面。这里的食物事实上都是假的。这里的学生正在上的是一个为期五天的课程，来学习如何让餐厅红火起来，如何当老板。

在第一场实境模拟中，到处大排长队，到处是失望的顾客和慌慌张张的经理。接着点餐变得更加复杂，目的是要测试点餐柜台运作的极限。

汉堡大学女性讲师
你觉得这会如何影响你的顾客？

女学生
每个人都很不高兴。你只看到经理跑来跑去，但却没帮到忙。这比其他任何场面都要混乱。

《CNN 钱线》芭比·哈洛
回到课堂上。

汉堡大学女性讲师
好，我的团队们。我们可以谈谈刚刚发生了什么事吗？

男学生
他们态度很亲切，但我无法很快拿到我的餐点。

4. **hum** [hʌm] *v.* 繁忙；活跃
The workshop hummed with activity.

5. **groom** [grum]
v. 培养；训练；做好准备
Dan's father groomed him for a job in his law firm.

6. **simulation** [ˌsɪmjəˈleʃən]
n. 模拟

7. **flustered** [ˈflʌstəd]
adj. 慌张的；激动不安的
Ben gets flustered when talking to attractive women.

8. **back and forth** 来来回回
The ants marched back and forth from their nest to the food source.

9. **chaotic** [keˈɑtɪk]
adj. 混乱的；杂乱的
Public transportation hubs can be chaotic on the day before a national holiday.

FEMALE STUDENT

It was just really busy. It kept holding, so she kept sending everybody on break.

POPPY HARLOW, CNN MONEY

So they try again, this time, applying[10] the lessons of the classroom to cut the chaos in the kitchen.

Okay, here we go.

FEMALE HAMBURGER UNIVERSITY INSTRUCTOR

Hi, would you like to try an iced mocha today?

POPPY HARLOW, CNN MONEY

I would like Cinnamon[11] Melts; a bacon, egg and cheese bagel; a sausage egg McMuffin, and a hash brown.[12] I'm just really in a rush.

Pretty fast so far. Let's see if they get the order right.

MALE STUDENT

We have a bacon, egg and cheese bagel; we have a Cinnamon Melts and we have one hash brown.

POPPY HARLOW, CNN MONEY

And what about the sausage McMuffin?

MALE HAMBURGER STUDENT

Sausage egg muffin?

POPPY HARLOW, CNN MONEY

C'mon, guys. They said it was in a rush. Let's go.

MALE STUDENT

And I got it for you.

女学生

实在是很忙。流程老是不顺利，所以她就一直叫每个人暂离岗位去帮忙。

《CNN 钱线》琶比·哈洛

所以他们要再试一次，这次他们将应用课堂所学，减少厨房的混乱。

好了，我们走吧。

汉堡大学女讲师

你好，请问你今天想尝尝冰摩卡吗？

《CNN 钱线》琶比·哈洛

我想要糖浆肉桂卷、培根蛋起司堡、猪柳麦满分和一份薯饼。我真的在赶时间。

到目前为止都相当快速。来看看他们是不是能正确备餐。

男学生

一个培根蛋起司堡、一个糖浆肉桂卷和一份薯饼。

《CNN 钱线》琶比·哈洛

猪柳麦满分呢？

男学生

猪柳麦满分？

《CNN 钱线》琶比·哈洛

大家加油。他们说赶时间。动作快点。

男学生

我帮你拿来了。

---

⑥ 从"汉堡"大学看麦当劳的员工训练哲学

麦当劳汉堡大学

创立

1961 年 Fred Turner 于伊利诺伊州 Elk Grove Village 分店地下室开始员工培训。

现址

2815 Jorie Boulevard, Oak Brook, Illinois，1983 年迁至麦当劳企业总部所在地。

占地

建筑 1.2 万平方米，校园 32 万平方米。

设施

13 间教室，12 间互动团体教室，3 间实验厨房，1 座可容纳 300 人的礼堂（auditorium）。

师资

30 位驻校教授（resident professor），19 位全职指导员，可用 28 种语言授课。

学生

每年超过 5000 人，毕业的店长、经理、从业者超过 8 万人。

海外分校

2010 年 3 月于中国上海成立。

POPPY HARLOW, CNN MONEY

That was a minute and 30 seconds.

And Hamburger University isn't a new thing. It was founded all the way back in 1961 in the basement of an ~~Ohio~~ [Illinois] McDonald's with just 14 people. As I said, about a quarter of a million have graduated since then. And this is no joke. McDonald's says Hamburger University is the key to its success over the years. Major companies like Target and Wal-Mart have sent their executives[13] in to see just how McDonald's trains its employees and some colleges even give credit[14] to students who attend Hamburger U. What this shows us is there's a lot more behind those golden arches than we knew before.

《CNN 钱线》芭比·哈洛

总共花了一分三十秒。

汉堡大学不是新成立的机构。它早在 1961 年就成立于伊利诺伊州的一家麦当劳地下室。刚开始只有 14 个人。如同我之前说的，从那时候开始，大约有 25 万人从这里毕业。这可不是开玩笑的，麦当劳表示汉堡大学是这些年来的成功关键。许多大公司如塔吉特、沃尔玛都曾派主管人员来观摩麦当劳是如何训练员工的。有些学院甚至承认汉堡大学学生的学分。这告诉我们，在麦当劳的金色拱门里还有许多我们以前不知道的事。

Notes & Vocabulary

no joke
不是开玩笑；正经的
joke 是指"玩笑；笑话"，口语中常说 it is no joke 加上 that 从句，表示"某事不是开玩笑的；是认真严肃的"，no joke 也可换成 not a joke。

- It's no joke that most life-threatening accidents happen in the home.
  说真的，大部分威胁生命的意外都发生在家里。

相似词
= no laughing matter

the key to success
成功的诀窍
key "钥匙"引申有"关键；要诀"的意思，后面用介词 to 加上事物。

- For Jeff, persistence has been the key to success.
  对杰夫来说，勤奋不懈就是成功的诀窍。

13. **executive** [ɪgˈzɛkjətɪv]
    n. 管理人员；主管

14. **credit** [ˈkrɛdɪt]
    n. 学分；认可

行业之道　品牌哲学　财经内幕　商海拾趣　环球生活

麦当劳简史

1940

Richard McDonald 和 Maurice McDonald 兄弟继承父亲的汉堡店，迁到加州圣博纳迪诺 66 号公路旁开设了第一家 McDonald's 餐厅。

1953

Nei Fox 获授权在亚利桑那州凤凰城开了第一家加盟店，以金色双拱为标志。

1961

注册金色双拱（golden arches）标志。

1967

巨无霸（Big Mac）问世。

1950   1960

1948

建立 Speedee Service System，奠定往后的快餐经营模式。

1955

加盟者 Ray Kroc 创立 McDonald's Systems, Inc. 成为进军全美及全球的推手。

1963

麦香鱼（Filet-O-Fish）问世，吉祥物（mascot）麦当劳叔叔（Ronald McDonald）登场，由 Willard Scott 扮演。

06-F.MP3 / 06-S.MP3 ▎ *Hamburgerology 101*

1975
第一家汽车餐厅（Drive Thru）在亚利桑那州成立。

1979
推出快乐儿童餐（Happy Meal）。

1993
M 首先在澳大利亚和墨尔本以概念店形式试营业。

2003
推出"I'm lovin' it."标语及广告。

1970

1990

2000

1973
吉士蛋麦满分（Egg McMuffin）问世。

1977
开始推出早餐。

1980
推出麦香鸡（McChincken）和麦乐鸡块（Chicken McNuggets）。

行业之道
品牌哲学
财经内幕
商海拾趣
环球生活

55

60 Years in the Fast Lane

Racing and Sports Car Legend[1] Ferrari Celebrates Landmark[2]

图片提供 :Reuters

CNN ANCHOR

Well, the prancing[3] black stallion[4] of Italy's luxurious[5] car industry turns 60 this year. The Ferrari is now being sold in 52 markets around the world and exports almost 90 percent of the cars it builds.

CNN ANCHOR

So what does the maker of arguably[6] the world's most iconic[7] car do to mark this landmark event? CNN's Alessio Vinci joined Ferrari lovers in Italy as they celebrate Ferrari's naught[8] to 60.

ALESSIO VINCI, CNN CORRESPONDENT

There is perhaps no better way to celebrate Ferrari's 60th anniversary than catching a ride with Michael Schumacher, the seven-time Formula One

07-F.MP3
07-S.MP3

名人小档案 ▼ 迈克尔·舒马赫

生日：1969 年 1 月 3 日

身高：174 厘米

体重：75 千克

出生地：德国 Hurth–Hermuhlheim

居住地：瑞士 Vufflens

婚姻状况：已婚（妻 Corina、女 Gina Maria、
　　　　　子 Mick）

方程式赛车辉煌战绩：

总冠军次数（championship）：7 次

分站冠军次数（race victories）：91 次

单圈最快次数（fastest laps）：76 次

杆位次数（pole positions）：68 次

生涯积分（points scores）：1369 分

Michael Schumacher

CNN 主播

意大利豪华汽车产业的奔腾黑马，今年已经
年满 60 岁。法拉利现在销往世界上 52 个国
家的市场，而且生产的车辆将近 90% 都外
销至其他国家。

CNN 主播

那么，对于这种堪称世界上最著名的车辆，
制造商是怎么去庆祝这个里程碑式的事件呢？
CNN 的亚勒席欧·芬奇，在意大利加入了法
拉利车迷的行列，共同庆祝法拉利从零岁到
60 岁的成就。

CNN 特派员 亚勒席欧·芬奇

庆祝法拉利 60 周年，最完美的方式应该就
是和迈克尔·舒马赫同乘一辆车了吧。这位
7 度赢得一级方程式冠军的赛车手在去年退

Notes & Vocabulary

1. legend [ˈlɛdʒənd]
   n. 传奇；传说

2. landmark [ˈlændˌmɑrk]
   n. 重大事件；里程碑

3. prance [ˈpræns] *v.* (马）腾跃
   The pony pranced across the parade
   ground.

4. stallion [ˈstæljən] *n.* 种马

5. luxurious [lʌgˈʒuriəs]
   adj. 奢侈的；豪华的
   Wendy spent the weekend at a
   luxurious resort.

6. arguably [ˈɑrgjuəblɪ]
   adv. 可以算是

7. iconic [aɪˈkɑnɪk] *adj.* 著名的
   The shirt was printed with the clothing
   company's iconic logo.

8. naught [nɔt]
   n. 无；不存在

行业之道 品牌哲学 财经内幕 商海拾趣 环球生活

champion, who retired last year after beating[9] nearly every record in the business.

As we drove in Ferrari's hometown racetrack trailed[10] by hundreds of fans, Schumacher says words alone can't describe the feeling of driving such cars—the power, the speed, of course, but there is something else.

MICHAEL SCHUMACHER, RETIRED FORMULA ONE CHAMPION
The other teams, they have maybe a group of fans. We have a whole country.

ALESSIO VINCI, CNN CORRESPONDENT
At the core[11] of this bond[12] between Ferrari and its obsessed[13] public is a passion for beauty, style and elegance; a long history of victories, but also tragedies; and a company that managed to produce over the years hundreds of models, each appearing unique in its own way, all sharing a common thread.[14]

MALE FERRARI FAN
That's what [I love] about Ferrari.

MALE FERRARI FAN
It's a racing car, but it's built for the road.

FEMALE FERRARI FAN
And the noise.

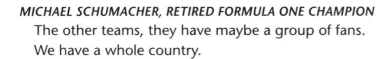

役。他在职业生涯中几乎打破了赛车场上的所有纪录。

我们开车驶过法拉利故乡的赛车道，道旁挤满了数以百计的车迷。舒马赫说，开这种车的感觉是言语无法描述的——那种马力，那种速度。当然，还有其他的东西。

一级方程式退役冠军 迈克尔·舒马赫
其他车队也许有一群车迷，我们却有一整个国家的车迷。

CNN 特派员 亚勒席欧·芬奇
法拉利和他们的忠实车迷彼此之间的共通处就是有激情、追求美、追求不凡的格调与高雅的品位。法拉利拥有一长串的胜利记录，但也经历过不少困境。这家公司多年来已经生产过上百款车，每一款都有其独特之处，但又具有共同的风格。

法拉利男车迷
这就是我最爱法拉利的地方。

法拉利男车迷
法拉利是赛车，可是也适合在一般道路上行驶。

法拉利女车迷
还有那种声音。

Notes & Vocabulary

9. **beat** [bit] *v.* 击败；胜过
The stock's performance beat all expectations.

10. **trail** [trel] *v.* 跟随；追踪
The software company trailed its competition.

11. **core** [kɔr] *n.* 核心；精髓

12. **bond** [bɑnd] *n.* 联结；联系

13. **obsessed** [əb`sɛst] *adj.* 着迷的
Ben is obsessed with video games.

14. **thread** [θrɛd] *n.* 贯穿的东西

行业之道｜品牌哲学｜财经内幕｜商海拾趣｜环球生活

ALESSIO VINCI, CNN CORRESPONDENT
Well, other Ferrari lovers would call it music, but what about it?

FEMALE FERRARI FAN
It's loud.

ALESSIO VINCI, CNN CORRESPONDENT
The man behind Ferrari's success today is Luca Cordero di Montezemolo. With Schumacher, he brought home five consecutive[15] world championships between 2000 and 2004, but when he took over the company in the early 1990s, Ferrari had not won a season in 21 years. Its fabulous[16] cars, meanwhile, remained[17] unsold.

LUCA CORDERO DI MONTEZEMOLO, FERRARI PRESIDENT
I said listen, this is terrible for us because we are for exclusivity.[18] I always say Ferrari is like a good-looking woman. Not only good, you have to desire[19] her, so wait.

ALESSIO VINCI, CNN CORRESPONDENT
The formula for success was simple—slow down production to the point need became greater than supply and boost[20] the luxury feel for the brand. It worked, and today thousands from all over the world drove their own Ferraris back to this small town in northern Italy, led by today's champions driving yesterday's cars, with a look very much into the future.

CNN 特派员 亚勒席欧·芬奇

其他法拉利车迷会把这种声音称为音乐，可是这种声音究竟如何呢？

法拉利女车迷

声音很大。

CNN 特派员 亚勒席欧·芬奇

现在，法拉利成功的推手是蒙泰泽莫洛。他在 2000 年至 2004 年间与舒马赫合作，连续抱回了五座世界冠军奖杯。不过，他在 20 世纪 90 年代初期接下这家公司的时候，法拉利已经连续 21 年不曾得过冠军，它绝佳的车辆在当时也一直卖不出去。

法拉利总裁 蒙泰泽莫洛

当时我说：听着，这对我们而言实在太糟糕了，因为我们应该是独一无二的。我总说法拉利就像是美貌女子，不只是好而已，还必须让人产生追求她的欲望。所以，就让顾客等吧。

CNN 特派员 亚勒席欧·芬奇

成功的公式很简单——放慢生产速度，让需求大于供给，借此提升这个品牌的奢华感。这个策略确实奏效。今天，世界各地数以千计的法拉利车主都开着他们自己的爱车回到了意大利北部的这座小镇。引领在前的是今日的冠军，他开着昨日的车辆，看起来却深具未来意义。

Notes & Vocabulary

... to the point
到了……的程度

point 可当做"观点；重点"等，在这里 point 解释为"程度；地步"。文中的 slow down production to the point ... 是说将生产法拉利的速度尽量减缓，直到市场的需求高过生产的量。

· Cindy was exhausted to the point that she could walk no further.
辛迪已经累得再也走不下去了。

延伸学习

词组 to the point 也可解释为"中肯的；切中要害的"。

· Helen's memo to the office staff was concise and to the point.
海伦交代给办公室员工的备忘录非常简明扼要。

15. **consecutive** [kənˈsɛkjətɪv]
    adj. 连续不断的
    The team won three consecutive championships.

16. **fabulous** [ˈfæbjələs] *adj.* 极好的
    Jenny wore a fabulous gown to the party.

17. **remain** [rɪˈmen] *v.* 保持；仍是
    Mr. Johnson remains Seth's favorite teacher.

18. **exclusivity** [ˌɛkskluˈsɪvəti]
    n. 独有；独一无二

19. **desire** [dɪˈzaɪr] *v.* 渴望
    Alex desires a change in his career.

20. **boost** [bust] *v.* 提高；增进
    The good publicity boosted the star's profile.

行业之道

品牌哲学

财经内幕

商海拾趣

环球生活

Ferrari S.P.A.

创始

1947 年 / 恩佐·法拉利（Enzo Ferrari ）

总部

意大利的玛拉连诺小镇（ Maranello ）

总裁

卢卡·迪·蒙泰泽莫洛（Luca Cordero di Montezemolo ）

恩佐·法拉利在 1929 年创办 Scuderia Ferrari 车队，当时他只是业余车手（amateur drivers ）的赞助人（ sponsor ），并无意制造跑车。自恩佐改装阿尔法·罗密欧（Alfa Romeo ）的跑车成功参与赛事后，至 1938 年被阿尔法聘请为赛车部主管。

法拉利汽车的发展

· 1940 年，阿尔法·罗密欧被墨索里尼（Benito Mussolini ）的法西斯（Fascist ）政府收编政权之下，恩佐在该年制造出第一部法拉利跑车 Tipo 815 ，在 Mille Miglia 赛事上正式亮相。

· 1947 年，恩佐制造出第一部非赛事使用的法拉利汽车 125 S ，主要是为了声援（fund ）他的 Scuderia 车队。

· 如今，菲亚特汽车集团（FIAT Group）拥有法拉利汽车 85%的股权，Mubadala 拥有 5% ，恩佐的儿子拥有 10%。

行业之道 品牌哲学 财经内幕 商海拾趣 环球生活

A Hot Slice of the Truth

Domino's Introduces
New Pizza While
Trashing[1] the Old

图片提供：Reuters

WOLF BLITZER, THE SITUATION ROOM
　Trashing your own product—it's a Moost Unusual way to sell pizza. Here's CNN's Jeanne Moos.

JEANNE MOOS, CNN CORRESPONDENT
　It may be the weirdest ad campaign[2] ever—Domino's bashes[3] itself.

KAREN KAISER, DOMINO'S MARKETING DIRECTOR
　The worst excuse[4] for pizza I've ever had.

JEANNE MOOS, CNN CORRESPONDENT
　It's either the worst or the best excuse for an ad campaign.

08-F.MP3
08-S.MP3

《时事观察室》主持人 沃夫·布里策尔
　　狂骂自家的产品，这是《莫斯不一样》节目的卖比萨方式，请看吉妮·莫斯的报道。

CNN 特派员 吉妮·莫斯
　　这恐怕是有史以来最怪异的广告活动——达美乐大骂自己。

达美乐比萨营销总监 凯伦·凯瑟
　　这是我吃过的最差的比萨。

CNN 特派员 吉妮·莫斯
　　就广告活动来说，这不是最差的广告，就是最好的广告。

Notes & Vocabulary

1. **trash** [træʃ] *v.* 谴责；抨击
   The critic trashed the play saying it was unwatchable.

2. **ad campaign** [æd] [kæm`pen]
   （一系列）广告活动

3. **bash** [bæʃ] *v.* 严厉批评
   Craig bashed his hometown baseball team because of their long losing streak.

4. **excuse** [ɪk`skjuz]
   n. 借口；拙劣的东西

行业之道 ｜ 品牌哲学 ｜ 财经内幕 ｜ 商海拾趣 ｜ 环球生活

UNIDENTIFIED FEMALE FOCUS GROUP PARTICIPANT
Domino's pizza crust,[5] to me, is like cardboard.[6]

MEREDITH BAKER, DOMINO'S EMPLOYEE
The sauce tastes like ketchup.

JEANNE MOOS, CNN CORRESPONDENT
Domino's is dissing[7] their old pizza—the one they've been selling us for nearly 50 years.

PATRICK DOYLE, DOMINO'S PRESIDENT
There comes a time when you know you've got to make a change.

JEANNE MOOS, CNN CORRESPONDENT
Now Domino's has a new pizza and they say the only thing that's the same…

RUSSELL WEINER, CHIEF MARKETING OFFICER
It's still round.

JEANNE MOOS, CNN CORRESPONDENT
All that stuff about their old pizza tasting like cardboard…

SAM FAUSER, DOMINO'S HEAD CHEF
I mean that hits you right in the heart.

Notes & Vocabulary

焦点团体参与者 不知名女子

对我来说达美乐比萨的饼皮就像厚纸板一样。

达美乐员工 梅瑞迪斯·贝克

酱汁的味道好像番茄酱。

CNN 特派员 吉妮·莫斯

达美乐骂的是他们从前卖的比萨——就是他们卖了将近 50 年的那种。

达美乐总裁 派屈克·多易尔

你总会碰到知道自己非得做出改变的时刻。

CNN 特派员 吉妮·莫斯

达美乐推出了新的比萨，他们说唯一和从前一样的是……

营销长 罗素·伟纳

它还是圆的。

CNN 特派员 吉妮·莫斯

那么有关他们以前的比萨吃起来像厚纸板这件事……

达美乐主厨 山姆·佛塞

这话真是让人伤心透了。

5. crust [krʌst] *n.* 糕饼酥皮；饼皮

6. cardboard [ˈkɑrd͵bɔrd] *n.* 硬纸板；厚纸板

7. dis [dɪs] *v.* 侮辱；看不起
Jack dissed Elaine's taste in music.

行业之道 ｜ 品牌哲学 ｜ 财经内幕 ｜ 商海拾趣 ｜ 环球生活

JEANNE MOOS, CNN CORRESPONDENT

...which prompted[8] one critic to post: "What kills[9] me is why does the guy who is the head chef in the Domino's commercial still have a job?"

Stephen Colbert reviewed[10] the new pizza...

STEPHEN COLBERT, THE COLBERT REPORT

Is that pizza or did an angel just give birth in my mouth?

JEANNE MOOS, CNN CORRESPONDENT

...while noting the honesty of the ad campaign.

STEPHEN COLBERT, THE COLBERT REPORT

Domino's old pizza's cheese did not taste good, had no aroma,[11] was not cheese.

JEANNE MOOS, CNN CORRESPONDENT

But now, they say...

SAM FAUSER, DOMINO'S HEAD CHEF

We've got shredded[12] cheese. Cheese. It's cheese.

JEANNE MOOS, CNN CORRESPONDENT

Imagine saying this about the pizza you've been selling forever.[13]

KAREN KAISER, DOMINO'S MARKETING DIRECTOR

Totally void[14] of flavor.

CNN 特派员 吉妮·莫斯

这让一位美食评论家发布了以下内容：“我受不了的是，达美乐广告里的主厨怎么还没被炒鱿鱼？”

史帝芬·科伯特对新比萨做出了评论。

《科伯特报告》主持人 史帝芬·科伯特

那是比萨吗？还是我的口中刚有位天使诞生了？

CNN 特派员 吉妮·莫斯

同时指出该广告的诚实之处。

《科伯特报告》主持人 史帝芬·科伯特

达美乐旧款比萨的奶酪不好吃，没有香味，称不上是奶酪。

CNN 特派员 吉妮·莫斯

但是现在，他们却说……

达美乐主厨 山姆·佛塞

我们有刨碎的奶酪丝了。奶酪，是奶酪。

CNN 特派员 吉妮·莫斯

想象一下，对于你卖了一辈子的比萨讲出这种话。

达美乐比萨营销总监 凯伦·凯瑟

完全没味道。

Notes & Vocabulary

8. **prompt** [prɑmpt] *v.* 促使；激起
   David's back pain prompted him to see a doctor.

9. **kill** [kɪl] *v.* 使痛苦；使受折磨
   It killed me that we missed our flight by just minutes.

10. **review** [rɪˋvju] *v.* 评论
    The local paper reviewed Donnie's play.

11. **aroma** [əˋromə] *n.* 香味

12. **shred** [ʃrɛd] *v.* 切碎
    The chef shredded lettuce for the salad.

13. **forever** [fəˋrɛvə]
    adv. 没完没了地；一直地

14. **void** [vɔɪd] *adj.* 缺乏的
    Rachel's band is totally void of talent.

行业之道 品牌哲学 财经内幕 商海拾趣 环球生活

JEANNE MOOS, CNN CORRESPONDENT

So how's the new stuff? It doesn't taste like cardboard.

UNIDENTIFIED FEMALE

It's not gourmet[15] pizza, but it's—it's good pizza.

UNIDENTIFIED MALE

I like the old one better.

UNIDENTIFIED MALE

Delicious.

UNIDENTIFIED MALE

It's kind of like we suck,[16] but now we're a little bit better.

JEANNE MOOS, CNN CORRESPONDENT

Uh-huh.

UNIDENTIFIED MALE

But you still suck, I think. Sorry, but you do suck.

JEANNE MOOS, CNN CORRESPONDENT

Hey, don't tell Honey that. Yo quiero Domino's Pizza.

CNN 特派员 吉妮·莫斯

新的比萨如何？味道不像厚纸板。

不知名女子

不算是顶级比萨，但是——算是好比萨。

不知名男子

我比较喜欢以前的比萨。

不知名男子

好吃。

不知名女子

有点像是在说以前我们很差劲，现在我们比较好一点了。

CNN 特派员 吉妮·莫斯

嗯。

不知名男子

但我觉得你们还是很差劲，抱歉，你们真的很差劲。

CNN 特派员 吉妮·莫斯

别这样跟小狗 Honey 说。我爱达美乐（注）。

注：出自美国墨西哥卷饼连锁店 Taco Bell 的知名广告，广告主角吉娃娃用西班牙语说，"Yo quiero Taco Bell!" "我爱 Taco Bell！"。这里记者因为拿比萨给狗试吃，所以借用该广告词。

Notes & Vocabulary

15. **gourmet** [ˋgurˏme] *n.* 美食家

16. **suck** [sʌk]
    v.【口】表现很糟；做得很差
    I admit it. I suck at poker!

行业之道

品牌哲学

财经内幕

商海拾趣

环球生活

HONEY'S OWNER
Easy, cowboy.

JEANNE MOOS, CNN CORRESPONDENT
But then Honey likes cardboard.

HONEY'S OWNER
No, no!

JEANNE MOOS, CNN CORRESPONDENT
Wait, where are you going with that?

UNIDENTIFIED FEMALE
I have a friend inside. She's hungry.

JEANNE MOOS, CNN CORRESPONDENT
You don't want the rest of it?

UNIDENTIFIED MALE
Nah.

JEANNE MOOS, CNN CORRESPONDENT
One more bite. You've got to have another bite.

UNIDENTIFIED FEMALE
Oh, no thank you.

UNIDENTIFIED FEMALE
I'm kosher.[17] I will go to hell because of a piece of pizza.

Honey 的主人

吃慢一点，小子。

CNN 特派员 吉妮·莫斯

不过 Honey 也喜欢旧的厚纸板比萨。

Honey 的主人

不，不行！

CNN 特派员 吉妮·莫斯

等一下，你要把那片比萨拿到哪里？

不知名女子

我有个朋友在里面。她肚子饿了。

CNN 特派员 吉妮·莫斯

你不想要剩下的比萨吗？

不知名男子

不了。

CNN 特派员 吉妮·莫斯

再吃一口。你非得再吃一口不可。

不知名女子

不了，谢谢你。

不知名女子

我遵守犹太饮食教规。吃一片比萨我就会下
地狱的。

17. **kosher** [ˋkoʃɚ]
   adj. 合乎（犹太教食物）规定的
   Simon's orthodox Jewish faith requires
   him to eat only kosher foods.

JEANNE MOOS, CNN CORRESPONDENT
Domino's marketing director says the new ad campaign shows…

RUSSELL WEINER, CHIEF MARKETING OFFICER
How much America embraces[18] the truth.

JEANNE MOOS, CNN CORRESPONDENT
Yep. Remember what they said about the old pizza before calling it cardboard?

UNIDENTIFIED MALE
Taste the new buttery[19] crust. Smell the garlic.

JEANNE MOOS, CNN CORRESPONDENT
And now the totally new and improved pie.

ROXANE SWAMBA, PIZZA CHEF
Buttery crust with some garlic.

JEANNE MOOS, CNN CORRESPONDENT
It sure had New Yorkers flocking[20] to try it.

SAM FAUSER, DOMINO'S HEAD CHEF
We improved everything—40 percent more herbs in the sauce.

CNN 特派员 吉妮·莫斯

达美乐的营销总监表示，新的广告活动显示……

营销长 罗素·伟纳

美国人有多爱听实话。

CNN 特派员 吉妮·莫斯

的确。还记得他们说以前的比萨像厚纸板之前说了些什么吗？

不知名男子

尝尝新的奶油香饼皮，闻闻蒜香。

CNN 特派员 吉妮·莫斯

现在推出全新的、口味改良的饼皮了。

比萨厨师 罗珊·史旺巴

奶油饼皮，带一点蒜香。

CNN 特派员 吉妮·莫斯

新的比萨确实让纽约客蜂拥前来品尝。

达美乐主厨 山姆·佛塞

我们改良了每一样东西，酱汁里的香料增加了40%。

18. **embrace** [ɪm`bres]
    v. 欣然接受（思想、建议等）
    U.S. audiences have embraced many television shows imported from Britain.

19. **buttery** [`bʌtərɪ]
    adj. 含奶油的
    The bread has a delicious buttery flavor.

20. **flock** [flɑk] *v.* 群集；蜂拥
    Customers flocked to the new donut shop.

How to Make a Toast Pizza
吐司比萨简单做

1. 准备一片吐司或是切片（sliced）法国面包（french bread）。

2. 用烤箱将面包烤到焦黄（brown）并略呈酥脆（crisp）的状态。

3. 在烤好的面包上均匀涂抹意大利面酱（spaghetti sauce）。

4. 在面包上放上自己想要的配料。（topping）

5. 将切碎（shred）的奶酪放在配料上。

6. 将面包送入烤盘，看到奶酪融化（melt）就完成了。

行业之道 品牌哲学 财经内幕 商海拾趣 环球生活

Pop Icon

Putting the Fizz[1] in the Coca-Cola Brand

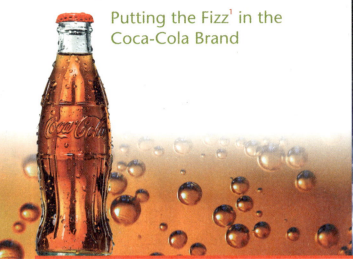

图片提供：The Coca-Cola Company

MONITA RAJPAL, ICON

For 125 years, the signature[2] Coca-Cola bottle has been a familiar presence the world over, from billboards dominating urban landscapes to solitary[3] kiosks[4] in seemingly remote locations. The syrup[5] behind its success was the brainchild[6] of pharmacist[7] John Pemberton, who peddled[8] his wares[9] to a small drugstore in downtown Atlanta back in 1886.

09-F.MP3
09-S.MP3

Notes & Vocabulary

《经典人物》莫妮塔·拉吉波

　　125 年来，在世界各地都能够看到熟悉的招牌式可口可乐瓶，不论是在都市里处处可见的广告牌上，还是在偏远地区孤独矗立的售货亭里。促成可口可乐征服全球的是药剂师约翰·潘伯顿的点子。他在 1886 年向亚特兰大市区的一家小药局推销他的商品。

1. fizz [fɪz] *n.*（液体中的）气泡嘶嘶声
2. signature [ˈsɪɡnətʃə]
   n. 识别标志
3. solitary [ˈsɑləˌtɛrɪ]
   adj. 单个的；唯一的
   The solitary barn was the only building in the field.
4. kiosk [ˈkiˌɑsk]
   n.（出售报纸、饮料等的）售货亭
5. syrup [ˈsɪrəp] *n.* 糖水；糖浆
6. brainchild [ˈbrenˌtʃaɪld]
   n. 主意；发明
7. pharmacist [ˈfɑrməsɪst]
   n. 药剂师
8. peddle [ˈpɛdl]
   v. 挨户销售；兜售
   Several vendors peddled food by the boardwalk.
9. ware [wɛr]
   n.（小摊贩在街上或市场兜售的）商品

行业之道　品牌哲学　财经内幕　商海拾趣　环球生活

77

PHIL MOONEY, COCA-COLA ARCHIVIST

Pemberton had introduced a number of products into the marketplace. He had hair dyes. He had liver pills. He had all sorts of beauty aids. None of which had been successful. Coca-Cola was not his first attempt to manufacture and market a soft drink, but it became obviously his most successful. Unfortunately for Pemberton, he died just a year and a half after he introduced the product, so he never saw it to be a commercial success.

MONITA RAJPAL, ICON

Fortunately, a savvy[10] local businessman named Asa Candler saw its potential.

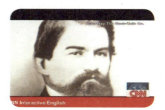

PHIL MOONEY, COCA-COLA ARCHIVIST

Candler really was everything that John Pemberton was not. He was a brilliant marketer. He understood how to promote new products and how to get consumers to try them. One of the things that Candler did that was different from what a lot of other marketers did is he used very good illustrators[11] and he used a lot of color in his advertising. He would get the very best lithographers[12] to do the calendars and the trays[13] that he was distributing. He would get really great illustrators to do the ads that would appear in the magazines of the day.

Notes & Vocabulary

可口可乐档案管理人 菲尔·穆尼

潘伯顿曾把不少产品引入市场。他做过染发剂、养肝丸，还有各种美容产品，但是都不成功。可口可乐不是他第一次尝试制造及营销的气泡饮料，但显然是他最成功的一款产品。只可惜，他推出这款产品之后一年半就去世了，所以根本没机会看到它获得商业上的成功。

《经典人物》莫妮塔·拉吉波

还好，当地有一位精明的商人，名叫艾萨·坎德勒，他看到了这款产品的潜力。

可口可乐档案管理人 菲尔·穆尼

坎德勒正好拥有潘伯顿所欠缺的一切特质。他是个绝佳的营销商，懂得如何推销新产品以及如何让消费者尝试。坎德勒采取了一种有别于其他营销业者的做法，就是雇用非常优秀的广告插画家，并且在广告中使用许多色彩。他找最好的印刷厂来印刷他发放的月历和文件盒。他也会找真正杰出的插画家绘制广告刊登在当时的杂志上。

10. savvy [ˈsævɪ]

   adj. 有见识的；通情达理的
   Julia is a savvy businesswoman.

11. illustrator [ˈɪləˌstretə]
   n. 插画家

12. lithographer [lɪˈθɑgrəfə]
   n. 平版印刷工

13. tray [tre] *n.* （办公桌上的）文件盒

行业之道 | 品牌哲学 | 财经内幕 | 商海拾趣 | 环球生活

MONITA RAJPAL, ICON

And so the company's marketing strategy was set. In 1899, Candler sold the rights to bottle[14] the beverage in the U.S., defining a franchising[15] business model and shaping an icon.

DAVID BUTLER, VP, GLOBAL DESIGN

When people think about our icon, the contour[16] bottle, that's a perfect balance of form and function. You know, it looks beautiful. It looks as good as it works. It's so functional, you can find it in the dark. That was actually the design brief back in 1916, to design something that you can find in the dark. And it [was] so recognizable that if it was shattered on the floor, you'd still be able to make out the contour.

MONITA RAJPAL, ICON

Over the years, Coke's advertising strategy has been a winning formula driven by the brand's ability to connect with consumers through strong storytelling. The harmonious[17] images of the Coca-Cola commercial belied[18] a fierce[19] battle of the brands as Pepsi called upon[20] the power of celebrity endorsements[21] and waged[22] war on the company's market share.

《经典人物》莫妮塔·拉吉波

这家公司的营销策略就这么确立了下来。1899 年，坎德勒在美国将这种饮料装瓶贩卖的权利售出，就此奠定了授权加盟的经营模式，并且塑造出一个代表性的图标。

全球设计副总裁 大卫·巴特勒

当人们想到我们代表性的曲线瓶时，会认为那是外形与功能的完美平衡。这个瓶子很好看，而且也很好用，非常具有功能性，即便在黑暗中也能找得到。当初在 1916 年的设计概要就是这么说的，要设计让人能够在黑暗中找得到的瓶子。此外，这个瓶子的辨识度很高，就算掉在地上摔碎了，也还是认得出外形。

《经典人物》莫妮塔·拉吉波

多年来，可口可乐一直有一套非常有效的广告策略，就是运用这个品牌以生动的故事连接消费者的能力。可口可乐广告的和谐形象掩饰了品牌之间的激烈竞争，百事可乐已经利用其对名人代言的号召力来挑起战争进攻可口可乐的市场占有率。

Notes & Vocabulary

14. **bottle** [ˈbɑtl]
   v. 把（液体）装入瓶中
   The perfume company bottles its premium fragrance in hand-blown glass containers.

15. **franchise** [ˈfrænˌtʃaɪz]
   v. 给予特权、经销权；加盟
   The fast food brand franchises outlets to local entrepreneurs.

16. **contour** [ˈkɑnˌtʊr] n. 外形；轮廓

17. **harmonious** [harˈmoniəs]
   adj. 友好和睦的；和谐的
   Bonnie and Ted have a harmonious relationship.

18. **belie** [bɪˈlaɪ] v. 掩饰；给人假象
   The man's shabby clothes belied the fact that he was quite wealthy.

19. **fierce** [fɪrs]
   adj. 凶狠的；狂暴的
   Greg is a fierce competitor.

20. **call upon** 邀请；要求
   Roger called upon his personal assistant to make arrangements for the party.

21. **endorsement** [ɪnˈdɔrsmənt]
   n. 背书；代言

22. **wage** [wedʒ]
   v. 开始；发动（战争、战斗等）
   The company waged war with its competitors.

行业之道　品牌哲学　财经内幕　商海拾趣　环球生活

WENDY CLARK, SR. V.P., MARKETING COMMUNICATIONS
Our position on the cola war is two strong competitors make for a more viable[23] industry. So we always want to compete against a healthy, strong, viable competitor or set of competitors, and ultimately I think the competitiveness in all of us as marketers enjoys that and makes us bring out sort of our best thinking and our best strategies into the marketplace.

DAVID BUTLER, VP, GLOBAL DESIGN
Now we're always thinking about competitive advantage no matter what you call it, war or what. The challenge with us is we operate on a huge scale.[24] We're local in 206 countries, in more countries than the U.N., so when we talk about scale, it's a kind of scale that no other company is dealing with.

MONITA RAJPAL, ICON
The success of the marketing strategies has rocketed[25] Coca-Cola to 1.6 billion drinks sold worldwide, a far cry from the nine drinks that an inventive pharmacist served in downtown Atlanta back in 1886.

营销传播资深副总 温迪·克拉克

我们在可乐战争上的立场是，两个强大的竞争者可以让产业更有活力。所以，我们总是希望与一个或一群健全、强大、稳健的对手一起竞争。身为营销业者，我想我们的好胜心终究会让我们乐在其中，也会促使我们把最好的想法和最佳的策略运用在市场上。

全球设计副总裁 大卫·巴特勒

不论你把商业竞争叫做战争还是什么，总之我们总是思考着竞争优势。我们面对的挑战就是我们的运营规模非常大。我们在 206 个国家都有当地的分公司，比联合国会员国还多。所以，一旦谈到规模，我们的规模是没有一家公司比得上的。

《经典人物》莫妮塔·拉吉波

营销策略的成功使得可口可乐在全世界狂卖了 16 亿罐。如今的可乐比起当初一位深具发明才华的药剂师在 1886 年亚特兰大市区端出的 9 杯饮料来，实在是不可同日而语。

Notes & Vocabulary

a far cry from
截然不同；有天壤之别

a far cry 原指 "长距离"，据说原指 19 世纪人们以叫喊声来测量远处敌人的位置，后来引申形容两件事物彼此间差距很大，即 "相去甚远" 的意思。

The movie star's glamorous lifestyle is a far cry from his humble childhood as the son of a poor farmer.
那位电影明星的生活光鲜亮丽，跟他身为贫农之子的寒微童年相距甚远。

23. **viable** [ˈvaɪəbl]
adj. 能独立生存的；可行的
For many high school graduates in the U.S., the military is a viable alternative to college.

24. **on a...scale** 以……的规模
The destruction caused by the storm was on a scale few had witnessed before.

25. **rocket** [ˈrɑkɪt]
v. (使)迅速成功；快速增长
The single rocketed to the top of the music charts.

Coca-Cola 大事记

1885
药剂师约翰·潘伯顿发明了一种含有可可碱和酒精的饮品，称为 Pemberton's French Wine Coca。

1892
坎德勒成立现今的可口可乐公司（The Coca-Cola Company）。

1894
可口可乐首次装瓶（bottle）发售。

1886
实施禁酒令（prohibition）后潘伯顿将他的发明改良成不含酒精的版本，取名 Coca-Cola，售价为一杯 5 美分，号称可治疗吗啡成瘾、消化不良（dyspepsia）、神经衰弱（neurasthenia）、头痛及性无能（impotence）等疾病。

1888
艾萨·坎德勒于 1887 年入股，来年组成 Coca Cola Company，当时有 4 家不同公司购得经销权销售各自版本的可口可乐。年底，坎德勒通过法律途径购得可乐配方独家所有权（exclusive rights）。

1915
为了与仿冒者区别而举办可乐瓶设计比赛，The Root Glass Company 的员工 Earl R. Dean 以可可亚豆荚（cocoa pod）为灵感设计出原型，再改良成直径较小的曲线瓶（contour bottle），被可口可乐公司相中量产。

1928

伍德鲁夫让可口可乐成为奥运会第一个广告赞助商（commercial sponsor），且赞助将持续至2020年。其他赞助过的运动赛事如 FIFA、MLB、NBA、NHL、NFL、NASCAR 等；同年研发推出了一盒 6 瓶装（six-pack）的包装。

1955

首次推出罐装（can）可乐；同年首次在户外墙上刊登绘图广告。

1982

可口可乐公司买下哥伦比亚电影公司，在其诸多电影中置入可乐产品形象。

1991

首度推出部分以回收塑料制成的瓶子，为业界创举。

1923

罗伯特·伍德鲁夫任总裁，将可口可乐推广到全世界。

1941

首次在广告上以 Coke 代称 Coca-Cola。

1978

获选唯一可在中华人民共和国贩卖罐装冷饮的公司。起初译作"蝌蝌啃蜡"，后来因销路不佳改名为"可口可乐"。

1985

首度更改配方推出 New Coke，虽受民众喜爱，但因大部分人怀念原来的口味而恢复旧配方；同年以 Coca-Cola Space Can 登上太空，成为第一个让航天员在舱内饮用的汽水。

图片提供：The Coca-Cola Company

行业之道｜品牌哲学｜财经内幕｜商海拾趣｜环球生活

 口味

可口可乐历年来曾推出过多种不同口味的产品，还有些是限定地区的特殊口味，如柠檬、朗姆、咖啡、覆盆子等，较为人所知的种类介绍如下：

1886
Coca-Cola
原味可口可乐

1982
Diet Coke /
Coke Light
健怡可乐

1983
Diet Coke
Caffeine-Free
无咖啡因健怡可乐

1985
Coca-Cola
Cherry
樱桃味可乐

2002
Coca-Cola
Vanilla
香草味可乐

2005
Coca-Cola
Zero
零卡可口可乐

Coca-Cola 经典广告

早期的月历广告，其中人物为女演员希尔妲·克拉克（Hilda Clark）。

1931 年首度使用圣诞老人作为广告主角。

1971 年推出多国年轻人在意大利一座山丘上合唱"I'd Like to Buy the World a Coke"的电视广告。

1993 年首度使用北极熊作为广告主角。

行业之道

品牌哲学

财经内幕

商海拾趣

环球生活

In His Blood

Harold McGraw
Heads[1] Family
Media Empire[2]

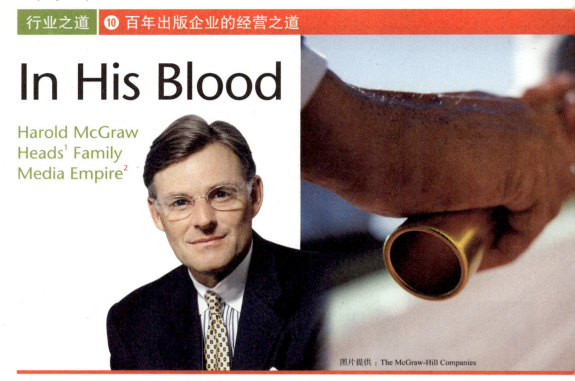

图片提供：The McGraw-Hill Companies

TODD BENJAMIN, THE BOARDROOM

They say business is in the blood, and what a pedigree.[3] Founded in 1888, The McGraw-Hill companies are made up of high-profile brands[4] like *Business Week* and Standard & Poor's. It's a leader in educational publishing and owns television stations. Presiding[5] over it all: Harold McGraw III.

名人小档案 ▼

Harold McGraw III

全名：Harold Terry McGraw III，
58 岁

职位：麦格劳·希尔公司总裁 (president)
兼首席执行官 (chief executive
officer)、商业圆桌 (Business
Roundtable) 主席

学历：1972 年塔夫斯大学
(Tufts University) 学士学位
1976 年宾州大学
(University of Pennsylvania)
商学硕士学位

《董事会》 陶德·本杰明

　　有人说经商要有祖传的天赋，那么这家公司
真该称得上是"名门世系"了。成立于 1888
年的麦格劳·希尔公司是由像《商业周刊》
和标准普尔这类高知名度的品牌所组成的公
司。该公司是教育出版界的领导者，并且
拥有自己的电视台。执掌这一切的人则是哈
洛·麦格劳·希尔三世。

Notes & Vocabulary

标题扫描

in one's blood 与生俱来；家传的

blood 是"血；血液；血脉"，in one's
blood 按照字面来看是"在某人血液之
中"的意思，引申为"某人与生俱来的能
力"或是"某人家传而来的"。

· Sports are in Jenny's blood.
运动的天分对珍妮来说是与生俱来的。

其他与 blood 连用的词组

in cold blood 冷血地；残忍地
· The security guard was murdered in cold
blood.
那名警卫被残忍地谋杀了。

bad blood 仇恨；宿怨
· There is bad blood between Alan and his
brother.
艾伦和他的哥哥一直痛恨彼此。

1. **head** [hɛd]
   v. 率领；站在⋯⋯的前头
   Sylvia heads a software company.

2. **empire** [ˈɛmˌpaɪr]
   n. 帝国；大企业

3. **pedigree** [ˈpɛdəˌgri] *n.* 名门世系

4. **brand** [brænd] *n.* 商标；品牌

5. **preside (over)** [prɪˈsaɪd]
   v. 管辖；指挥
   The judge presided over the hearing.

行业之道 品牌哲学 财经内幕 商海拾趣 环球生活

One of the challenges you had coming in was that back in 1993 when you were made president, you had a company that was very patriarchal.[6] It had been a family-run business. It was a type of culture that was jobs for life, and you had to change that culture. How did you do that?

HAROLD MCGRAW III, MCGRAW-HILL

It is never a nice situation when people are very comfortable and think that, you know, there's a certain umbrella[7] and there's a certain entitlement.[8] If you're going to be relevant[9] in the market place, and that is very very important. If you really are serious about the impacts you're going to make, then you've got to be able to make the changes, and internally,[10] you know, that's what we did. Talent is the most important thing that you've got—how you nurture[11] it, how you develop your talent,

您在接管公司时所面临的挑战之一是当您在 1993 年被任命为公司总裁时，贵公司是个非常父系的企业。它在过去一直是个家族企业，是那种奉行终身聘用制企业文化的公司，而您必须去改变这样的文化。您是如何做到的？

麦格劳·希尔公司　哈洛·麦格劳·希尔三世

当人们觉得很自在，认为有某种保障存在，并理应得到某些东西的时候，这绝非一种最佳的状态。如果你要在市场上发挥影响力，这一点又非常非常重要；如果你真的很在乎自己能发挥何种影响力，那么你就必须做出改变，而这就是我们在公司内部做的事。天赋是你能拥有的最重要的一件事，你要如

Notes & Vocabulary

the challenges you had coming in

这句话在文章中的意思是说"在一开始时出现的难题或挑战"，coming in 等于 from the beginning 。

coming 的惯用句型

have it coming 应得的报应
· Most people thought the businessman had it coming when he was convicted of fraud.
当那位企业家因欺诈被定罪时，大部人都认为他是罪有应得。

see it coming 预测某事来临
· When Julia was fired, she never saw it coming.
茱莉亚一点也没有预料到她会被开除。

6. **patriarchal** [ˌpetriˈɑrkl]
   adj. 父系的；族长制的
   Many cultures are patriarchal societies.

7. **umbrella** [ʌmˈbrɛlə]
   n. 保护伞；庇护

8. **entitlement** [ɪnˈtaɪtl̩mənt]
   n. 应得的权利

9. **relevant** [ˈrɛləvənt] *adj.* 有关的
   The witness' statements were not relevant to the case.

10. **internally** [ɪnˈtɜnəlɪ]
    adv. 内部的；内在的

11. **nurture** [ˈnɜtʃə]
    v. 养育；供给养分
    Tina nurtured the injured bird back to health.

行业之道　品牌哲学　财经内幕　商海拾趣　环球生活

how you career path your talent, how you look at challenges and all of those kind of things is really important. People matter,[12] and therefore, you know, your whole job really needs to be focused on the environment in which people work and the people that are actually doing the work.

TODD BENJAMIN, THE BOARDROOM
And when you look for certain qualities in your key lieutenants,[13] what are you looking for?

HAROLD MCGRAW III, MCGRAW-HILL
The first thing that I look for in any individual[14] is passion. You know: hey, you got energy? Are you alive and well? You know, do you get excited about things? Do you, you know, is life worth it and all those kind of things? And if you are, hey, we can go a lot of places with that. Skill sets you can learn; attitude you can't.

TODD BENJAMIN, THE BOARDROOM
So, did you always know that you would end up in business?

何去培育它，如何发展你的天赋，如何为你的天赋规划出一条可行的路，你如何看待挑战，这一切都很重要。人力是十分重要的资源，因此你必须把工作重点放在人们的工作环境上，放在实际从事那些工作的人身上。

《董事会》　托德·本杰明

您在选择您的重要高层干部时会特别注意哪些特质？

麦格劳·希尔公司　哈洛·麦格劳·希尔三世

我在看一个人的时候最想看到的是激情。你知道的，你有没有精神？你还活力四射吗？你会对事情感到兴奋吗？你的生命是否活得有价值等。如果你是这样的一个人，我们就能成就很多事。你可以学会做事的技巧，但态度是学不来的。

《董事会》　托德·本杰明

所以你一直都知道你终究会从商？

---

career path
职业途径
career path 原为名词，指"职业途径"，文中改变词性当动词用，是特例的用法。

· At age 50, Bonnie began a new career path as a writer.
波尼在 50 岁时转换新的职业成了作家。

12. **matter** [ˈmætə] *v.* 有关系；要紧
    How we treat people matters to those around us.

13. **lieutenant** [luˈtɛnənt]
    n. 副职官员；助理官员

14. **individual** [ˌɪndəˈvɪdʒʊəl]
    n. 个人；个体

行业之道　品牌哲学　财经内幕　商海拾趣　环球生活

HAROLD MCGRAW III, MCGRAW-HILL

I think so, yeah. You know, back at one point there was no question that I wanted to be an actor, and I wanted to, you know, think about the theater and all of that. I really love it. And I had a great professor and, you know, [he would] sit me down and say, "Do you know how competitive[15] it is, you know, to achieve all of these goals and everything? You know, you should really think, also, of the business world. It needs a lot of actors."

The McGraw-Hill Companies

成　立	1888 年成立于纽约
创办人	James H. McGraw / John A. Hill
总　部	纽约洛克菲勒中心 (Rockefeller Center)
领　域	教育、出版、传媒 (broadcasting)、财经与商业 (financial and business services)

麦格劳·希尔国际出版公司在商业企管、财经投资、医学、社会与自然科学、建筑、电机工程等出版领域享有盛名。*Business Week* 和 *Aviation Week* 等均为该公司出版的杂志。旗下子公司 (subsidiary) 有 **Standard & Poor's** 投资顾问公司、**J.D. Power and Associates** 市场调研公司等。

麦格劳·希尔公司　哈洛·麦格劳·希尔三世
我想是的。你知道吗，曾经一度我很确定自己想当一名演员，一心想着剧院这一类的事。我真的很爱演戏。过去我有一位很棒的教授郑重地跟我说："你知道戏剧这个行业的竞争有多激烈吗，知道要达到这些目标有多难吗？你应该好好想想从商这件事，商业界同样需要许多演员"。

Notes & Vocabulary

back at one point 曾经一度
point 是"点；特定的时刻"，back at one point 说的是"回到某一个点上"，也就是"曾经一度……"的意思。

· Back at one point, Jeff never imagined himself married with children.
曾经一度，杰夫从未想象自己会结婚生子。

其他与 point 连用的词组

the point of no return
无法回头的地步
· When the defector requested political asylum, he had passed the point of no return.
当投奔自由者寻求政治庇护时，就无法回头了。

at the point of something
某事即将发生的当口
· Lily was at the point of quitting her job.
莉莉当时几乎要提出辞职了。

sit someone down
郑重告诉某人
sit someone down 可直接照字面解释为"让某人坐下"，目的是让当事人专注聆听某件重要的事情，所以也表示"郑重告诉某人"的意思。

· The boss sat Mike down and told him that he better improve the quality of his work.
老板郑重地告诫麦克要改进工作表现。

15. **competitive** [kəmˈpɛtətɪv]
adj. 竞争的
Constant training gave the runner a competitive edge.

行业之道　品牌哲学　财经内幕　商海拾趣　环球生活

财经内幕

Jargon[1] Buster[2]: EBITDA

A Sneaky[3] Way to Hide a Company's Performance

图片提供：The McGraw-Hill Companies

ANJALI RAO, CNN ANCHOR

We are in the thick of a fresh earnings season. It's a deluge[4] of numbers, not to mention all the acronyms,[5] such as EBITDA. You might have read about that one, catchy[6] though it is. It stands for "earnings before interest, taxes, depreciation[7] and amortization.[8]" And if you don't understand what that means, well, you're not alone. Jim Boulden is on the jargon busting beat for us.

JIM BOULDEN, CNN CORRESPONDENT

Good morning, everyone. Today we'll be discussing an acronym that I'm sure you've all read about in the financial pages.

CNN 主播 安姿丽

我们适逢新的财务报表新鲜出炉之季，到处充斥着数字，更别提各式各样的缩写了，例如 "EBITDA"。你可能看到过这个缩写，这个词还蛮朗朗上口的。这个词指 "息前、税前、折旧和摊销前的获利"。你如果不了解这是什么意思，没关系，不是只有你不懂。吉姆·伯登要负责来帮我们破解术语。

CNN 特派员 吉姆·伯登

大家早安。今天我们要讨论一个缩略词，相信大家都在金融报道当中看到过。

Notes & Vocabulary

in the thick of...

深陷；在最激烈处

thick 当名词是 "最厚、最浓的部分"，引申为 "事物最活跃、最激烈之处"，in the thick of sth. 表示 "处于……最热烈的时候或状态"，有深陷其中的意思。

· The stockbroker likes to work **in the thick of** the action on the trading floor.
那位证券经纪人喜欢在交易所紧张忙碌的气氛中工作。

on the... beat 负责……领域

beat 当名词有 "常走的路线" 之意，可指 "巡逻的地段；辖区；管区"，也可表示记者 "经常负责采访的领域"，所以 on the... beat 就类似于中文 "跑……线" 的意思。

· The reporter began her career working **on the** police **beat**.
那位记者刚开始工作时是跑警察线的。

1. jargon [ˈdʒɑrgən]
   n. 术语；行话；黑话

2. buster [ˈbʌstə] *n.* 克星；破坏者

3. sneaky [ˈsnikɪ]
   adj. 偷偷摸摸的；鬼鬼祟祟的
   The accountant has several sneaky ways to hide taxable revenues.

4. deluge [ˈdɛljudʒ]
   n. 大量涌现；暴雨；洪水

5. acronym [ˈækrəˌnɪm]
   n. 首字母缩略词

6. catchy [ˈkætʃɪ]
   adj. 朗朗上口的；简单易计的
   Valerie heard a catchy song on the radio.

7. depreciation [dɪˌpriʃiˈeʃən]
   n. 折旧；贬值

8. amortization [əˌmɔrtəˈzeʃən]
   n. 摊销；分期偿还

行业之道 ｜ 品牌哲学 ｜ 财经内幕 ｜ 商海拾趣 ｜ 环球生活

KINDERGARTEN BOY
What's acronym?

JIM BOULDEN, CNN CORRESPONDENT
Well, it's sort of an abbreviation.[9]

KINDERGARTEN GIRL
What's abbreviation?

JIM BOULDEN, CNN CORRESPONDENT
Let's not worry about that now. EBITDA! That's earnings before interest, taxation,[10] depreciation and amortization.

KINDERGARTEN BOY
EBITDA.

KINDERGARTEN BOY
EBIKDA.

JIM BOULDEN, CNN CORRESPONDENT
It's a different way for potential investors to evaluate a company that isn't necessarily making a profit.

It was a particularly popular calculation[11] during the 1980s leverage buyout mania,[12] and during the dot-com bubble. It was often used by companies who thought it was a good idea to sell everything from books to holidays to antiques—even dog food—on the Internet. So, it might be used by a new company that's spending more money than it's making in a certain period.

幼儿园男童

缩略词是什么意思？

CNN 特派员 吉姆·伯登

就是一种缩写。

幼儿园女童

缩写是什么？

CNN 特派员 吉姆·伯登

现在先不谈这个问题。"EBITDA"！这个词代表息前、税前、折旧及摊销前的获利。

幼儿园男童

"EBITDA"。

幼儿园男童

"EBIKDA"。

CNN 特派员 吉姆·伯登

这是一种与众不同的评估方式，它可以让潜在的投资者评估一家不一定赚钱的公司。

这种计算方式在 20 世纪 80 年代的融资收购热潮与网络公司泡沫潮期间特别流行。它经常被那些认为在网上卖什么都很好的公司来使用——从书籍、度假行程到古董，甚至是狗粮。所以，新成立的公司如果在某段时期的支出多于收入，就可能会采用这种算法。

Notes & Vocabulary

9. **abbreviation** [əˌbriviˋeʃən]
   n. 缩写

10. **taxation** [tækˋseʃən]
    n. 税款；课税；税制

11. **calculation** [ˌkælkjuˋleʃən]
    n. 计算

12. **mania** [ˋmeniə] *n.* 狂热

leverage buyout
[ˋlɛvərɪdʒ][ˋbaɪˌaut] 融资收购

缩写为 LBO，又称为"杠杆收购"，是指收购者仅有少许资金，借由举债借入资本（**capital**）来收购（**acquire**）其他公司。犹如运用杠杆原理以很小的力量抬起重物一般。融资收购通常以即将收购的公司或未来的现金流（**cash flow**）作担保（**collateral**），但有时获利不如预期，因此风险极大。

行业之道 | 品牌哲学 | 财经内幕 | 商海拾趣 | 环球生活

Normally speaking, earnings relates to the income that comes through the door during a specific period. Pack it all up, then subtract[13] expenses, and you have…?

KINDERGARTEN BOY
Earnings?

JIM BOULDEN, CNN CORRESPONDENT
Precisely.[14] They're often the single most important determinant[15] of a stock's price, a hint of future dividends[16] and growth.

Now the thing that makes EBITDA a little controversial[17] is that it unravels[18] the earnings definition, pumping back in certain expenses as if they never happened, and that, class, is where the ITDA comes in: the interest, taxation, depreciation and…?

KINDERGARTEN BOY
Amortization?

JIM BOULDEN, CNN CORRESPONDENT
Exactly. It's like the company never paid interest on a bank loan, never paid any taxes, and it's like the company's assets never lost any natural value over time. And finally, amortization. It's like a company never has to account for a large chunk of[19] loans that it has to pay off.

KINDERGARTEN STUDENTS
It's not fair!

一般来说，获利和某一段时期的收入有关。把所有收入加起来，再减掉支出，结果就是？

幼儿园男童
获利吗？

CNN 特派员 吉姆·伯登
没错。获利经常是股价最重要的决定因素，暗示着未来的股息和成长。

"EBITDA" 之所以具有争议性，是因为它破坏了获利的定义。它把特定支出灌回获利里，仿佛这些支出不曾发生过一样。各位同学，这些支出就是所谓的 "ITDA"：利息、扣税、折旧和？

幼儿园男童
摊销？

CNN 特派员 吉姆·伯登
没错。这么做就像是公司从来不曾支付过银行贷款的利息，不曾支付过税金，而且公司的资产也不会随着时间流逝而贬值。至于摊销，则像是公司完全不必为自己必须偿还的高额贷款负起责任。

幼儿园学童
不公平！

Notes & Vocabulary

13. **subtract** [səb`trækt] *v.* 减；减去
William subtracted expenses from his projected income.

14. **precisely** [prɪ`saɪslɪ]
adv. 确实；的确；正是如此

15. **determinant** [dɪ`tɜmənənt]
n. 决定因素；决定条件

16. **dividend** [`dɪvə‚dɛnd]
n. 红利；股息；股利

17. **controversial** [‚kɑntrə`vɜʃəl]
adj. 引发争议的；争议性的
The controversial sculpture was removed from the library lobby.

18. **unravel** [‚ʌn`rævl]
v. 瓦解；解体；崩溃；展开
The play unraveled in the third act.

19. **a chunk of** 一大块的；一大部分的
The company donated a chunk of its profits to charity.

JIM BOULDEN, CNN CORRESPONDENT

Well, EBITDA is seen as an accounting gimmick[20] that can dress up a company's earnings, nor is it accepted under so-called generally agreed accounting principles. Even so, companies use EBITDA when other numbers aren't so rosy.[21]

Any questions?

EBITDA 息前税前折旧摊销前获利

Earnings 获利
= income − expenses Before
收入　不含 I.T.D.A. 的支出

Interest repayment
利息偿还

Tax deductions
税金扣除

Depreciation of assets
资产折旧

Amortization
(lump sum debt allocation)
摊销（整体借贷分期偿还）

11-F.MP3 / 11-S.MP3 | *Jargon Buster: EBITDA*

CNN 特派员 吉姆·伯登

"EBITDA" 被视为是一种会计把戏,可以用来美化一家公司的获利,而且所谓的一般公认会计原则也不允许这种做法。尽管如此,公司一旦发现自己的其他数据不太好看,就会启用 "EBITDA" 了。

有没有问题?

generally agreed accounting principles 一般公认会计原则

缩写为 GAAP ,又称 generally accepted accounting principles,指会计各环节在记录、计算和准备财务报表时皆须遵守的一些标准、常规(convention)、规定及原则,例如非补偿性原则(principle of non-compensation)规定财政信息应详细明列,不得直接以资产补偿负债、以营利补偿支出等。

dress up 美化

原本是"盛装;精心打扮"的意思,以事物为宾语时引申为"加以装饰;美化",好掩饰缺点,使之看起来更美好。

· Nelson dressed up for his date with Alice.
尼尔森为他和爱莉丝的约会盛装打扮。

· Maggie dressed up her presentation with several eye-catching graphics.
梅姬用许多醒目的图表强化她的报告。

20. **gimmick** [ˈɡɪmɪk]
n. 花招;把戏;噱头

21. **rosy** [ˈrozɪ] *adj.* 美好的;乐观的
Economists tempered their rosy predictions of economic recovery.

行业之道 ┃ 品牌哲学 ┃ 财经内幕 ┃ 商海拾趣 ┃ 环球生活

Stones from Blood

Conflict[1] Diamonds Continue to Flow from War-Torn West Africa

图片提供 :Reuters

CNN ANCHOR

A controversial[2] new film has opened here in the United States. *Blood Diamond* is set during the civil war[3] that engulfed[4] Sierra Leone in the 1990s, a war financed[5] by the trade in illicit[6] stones known as conflict diamonds. Femi Oke reports, though, that illegal diamond mining[7] does continue today.

12-F.MP3
12-S.MP3

Notes & Vocabulary

标题扫描

stones from blood

stones from blood 改写自惯用语 get blood out of a stone，字面解释是从石头中挤出血来，引申为"很困难；不可能"，例如无法从穷人身上榨出钱来。这里是运用 stone 当"钻石"的意思，指利比里亚的贫穷村民开采的钻石是用血汗换来的。

war-torn
饱受战火摧残的

war-torn 是"经战争摧残的"，torn 是动词 tear（撕裂；撕开）的过去分词当形容词用。这里是指西非的土地就像是被战火撕扯、撕裂一般饱受摧残。

· Charities sent aid to the war-torn country.
  慈善团体援助了那个饱受战火摧残的国家。

CNN 主播

　一部颇具争议性的电影在美国上映了。《血钻石》故事发生在 20 世纪 90 年代吞噬塞拉利昂的内战期间。这是一场由非法钻石（又称冲突钻石）买卖所资助的战争。但是根据费米·欧克的报道，非法钻石开采至今依旧持续进行着。

1. **conflict** [ˈkɑnflɪkt] *n.* 冲突

2. **controversial** [ˌkɑntrəˈvɜʃəl]
   adj. 有争议的
   The controversial novel was banned in some countries.

3. **civil war** [ˈsɪvl̩] [wɔr] 内战

4. **engulf** [ɪnɡʌlf] *v.* 吞没；卷入
   Civil war engulfed the country after it declared independence.

5. **finance** [faɪˈnæns]
   v. 提供资金
   The bank financed Dave's new business.

6. **illicit** [ɪˈlɪsɪt] *adj.* 非法的；违禁的
   The man was convicted of selling illicit drugs.

7. **mining** [ˈmaɪnɪŋ] *n.* 采矿；矿业

行业之道　品牌哲学　财经内幕　商海拾趣　环球生活

FEMI OKE, CNN CORRESPONDENT

Mabong Thandiong village in west Liberia is sitting on a secret. Just behind these houses, the women hustle[8] for gold and the men dig for diamonds, buried treasure for the taking. It's just hard work getting to it. But the location isn't the secret. It's the diamond mining that's undercover.[9]

LOMAX BOIMAR, DIAMOND MINER

You see today how we have sanctions[10] on diamonds. We are suffering in this country, there are no jobs. We just have to do this to survive.

FEMI OKE, CNN CORRESPONDENT

Lomax Boimar and his mining friends know all about the United Nations ban[11] on Liberia exporting diamonds.

ALFRED FAYIA, DEP. MIN., LANDS AND MINES

Well you see, you have to understand that Liberia, in Liberia mining is a culture, it's a tradition. You never stop people from mining.

You know this is not mega;[12] you know this [is] a little mining. We don't bother them much, because they have to live.

FEMI OKE, CNN CORRESPONDENT

Boakai Kanle lost both his parents in Liberia's civil war. He'd rather go to school than be a miner, but he has to eat. He says he sold his last diamond for US$2.

CNN 主播 费米·欧克

位于利比里亚西边的马朋·坦迪翁村的地底下有个秘密。就在这几间屋子后头，这些女人忙着采黄金，这些男人则是在挖掘钻石，这些宝藏就埋在地底下等着被人取走，要挖到这些宝藏是件苦差事，但这个藏宝之地并非秘密，真正的秘密是有人在这里开采钻石。

钻石开采工人 罗美克斯·波玛

现在大家都看到了钻石遭到禁运制裁的情况。我们在这个国家里受苦受难，没有工作机会。我们必须挖钻石才能生存下去。

CNN 主播 费米·欧克

罗美克斯·波玛和那些与他一起挖钻石的朋友很清楚联合国禁止利比里亚出口钻石这件事。

土地及矿业部部长 艾佛瑞·法义亚

你必须知道矿业在利比里亚是一种文化，一种传统。你阻止不了人们去挖矿。

你心里知道这么做无伤大雅，也知道这只是小规模的矿业。我们不太会去管他们，因为他们得活下去。

CNN 主播 费米·欧克

巴欧凯·坎里在利比里亚内战中失去了双亲。他宁愿上学，也不愿意去挖矿，但他必须填饱肚子。他说他的上一颗钻石卖了两美元。

Notes & Vocabulary

sit on a secret 坐守秘密

sit on 有"不可说；抑制"的意思，sit on a secret 在文中的意思是那些村民有着一个不可告人的秘密。这句话还可直接照字面解释，因为钻石矿埋藏在村落地底下，所以也就像是村民坐在这个秘密钻石矿上面。

· The company sat on information that their products were unsafe.
这家公司隐瞒了他们的产品不安全的事情。

此外

sit on 还有"延迟；迟迟不做决定"的意思。

· Ron sat on breaking up with his girlfriend long after their relationship turned sour.
朗与他的女友关系恶化已久，他仍迟迟不与她分手。

其他与 sit on 相关的词组

sit on one's hand 不插手；不干涉

· Kyle sat on his hands while his wife spent their savings.
凯尔的妻子挥霍他们的积蓄，他却完全不干涉。

8. **hustle** [ˈhʌsl] v. 赶紧做（某事）
Brenda hustled to make her sales quota.

9. **undercover** [ˌʌndəˈkʌvə] adj. 秘密从事的
Undercover agents arrested the kidnapper.

10. **sanction** [ˈsæŋkʃən] n. 国际制裁

11. **ban** [bæn] n. 禁止；禁令
Some countries imposed a ban on genetically modified food.

12. **mega** [ˈmɛgə] adj. 大量的
The company launched a mega construction project.

行业之道 | 品牌哲学 | 财经内幕 | 商海拾趣 | 环球生活

BOAKAI KANLE, DIAMOND MINER

I can get my chicken soup, buy rice, bananas and food for me to eat. I don't get money from them to get rich.

FEMI OKE, CNN CORRESPONDENT

The miners are working for subsistence[13] payments, because they're selling diamonds on the black market in Monrovia. Without sanctions, Boakai would be a lot wealthier.

Ambassador Ellen Loj is the chair of the U.N. Security Council's Committee for Liberian Sanctions.

AMBASSADOR ELLEN LOJ, U.N. COMMITTEE ON SANCTIONS

There's no doubt about it, the aim of the Security Council is to lift the sanctions as quickly as possible, but also to be sure that when we do it, the income benefit[s][14] the Liberian government and the Liberian people and not some illegal activities.

FEMI OKE, CNN CORRESPONDENT

Liberia's diamond sanctions will be reviewed[15] before the end of this year. In the meantime, a group of good-humored[16] miners continue to work illegally.

Is there anything in there? Is there anything in there? I'm not bringing you good luck. Nope.

钻石开采工人 巴欧凯·坎里

我可以买鸡汤、米、香蕉和食物来吃。我靠它们赚钱不是为了致富。

CNN 主播 费米·欧克

矿工们的工作酬劳仅够糊口，因为他们都是将钻石卖给蒙罗维亚的黑市。如果没有实施禁运制裁，巴欧凯会富有一些。

艾伦·罗杰大使是联合国安全理事会利比里亚禁运制裁委员会的主席。

联合国禁运制裁委员会大使 艾伦·罗杰

毫无疑问，安理会的目标是尽快解除禁运制裁，但同时也要确定当我们解除禁运制裁的时候，出售钻石的获益者是利比里亚政府和利比里亚人民，而非一些非法活动。

CNN 主播 费米·欧克

联合国将在今年底重新探讨利比里亚钻石的禁运制裁。与此同时，一群心情不错的矿工仍在继续非法地工作着。

挖到了吗？挖到了吗？我没能带给你好运。没办法。

13. **subsistence** [səb`sɪstəns]
    n. 生计；赖以活命的东西

14. **benefit** [`bɛnəfɪt] *v.* 得益；受惠
    The president's health care plan benefits low-income families.

15. **review** [rɪ`vju] *v.* 再检查；复审
    The team coach's position will be reviewed at the end of the season.

16. **good-humored** [`ɡʊd`hjuməd]
    adj. 心情愉快的；脾气好的
    Josh was good humored about the practical joke his friends played on him.

行业之道　品牌哲学　财经内幕　商海拾趣　环球生活

Liberia 利比里亚

正式国名：利比里亚共和国（Republic of Liberia）

总　　统：艾伦·强森·瑟利夫（Ellen Johnson-Sirleaf）

成 日 立：1847 年 7 月 26 日

首　　都：蒙罗维亚（Monrovia）

人　　口：约 328300 人

Security Council 安理会

安理会全名为"联合国安全理事会"（United Nations Security Council），为联合国 6 大主要机构（principal organs）之一。

根据《联合国宪章》（United Nations Charter）的宗旨及原则，安理会负有维持国际和平与安全的责任，是唯一有权采取强制行动的联合国机构。

安理会由 5 个常任理事国（permanent members）和 10 个非常任理事国（elected members）组成。

联合国 6 大机构

联合国大会	General Assembly
安全理事会	Security Council
经济及社会理事会	Economic and Social Council
托管理事会	Trusteeship Council
秘书处	Secretariat
国际法庭	International Court of Justice

行业之道 | 品牌哲学 | 财经内幕 | 商海拾趣 | 环球生活

The Gloves Come Off

Alan Greenspan Pulls No Political Punches in His New Memoir[1]

图片提供：美联储

CNN ANCHOR

Alan Greenspan's highly anticipated[2] memoir is on bookshelves today.

CNN ANCHOR

In it the ex-chairman of the Federal Reserve criticizes U.S. president George W. Bush, accusing[3] him of putting politics ahead of sound[4] economics.

13-F.MP3
13-S.MP3

Notes & Vocabulary

标题扫描

the gloves come off

以往西方男士想与人决斗时，会将手套脱下丢在地上，对方拾起表示接受挑战，因此"脱下手套"就用来表示"直接挑战"。格林斯潘向来言辞谨慎，被视为忠贞的共和党员，在书中却毫不客气地批评起共和党政府来。

· **The gloves came off** in the second presidential debate.
第二场总统选举辩论显得针锋相对。

相关用法

▶ take the gloves off

▶ with the gloves off

CNN 主播
艾伦·格林斯潘备受期待的回忆录（注）已在今天上市。

CNN 主播
这位美联储前主席在书中批评美国总统小布什，指控他将政治优先化，把经济的健全摆在第二位。

注：书名为 *The Age of Turbulence*: *Adventures in a New World*（Penguin, Sep. 17, 2007）。

1. **memoir** [ˈmɛmˌwɑr]
   n. 回忆录；自传

2. **anticipated** [ænˈtɪsəˌpatɪd]
   adj. 受期待的
   The author's highly anticipated second novel was released to rave reviews.

3. **accuse** [əˈkjus] *v.* 指控；谴责
   Eric's teacher accused him of cheating on a test.

4. **sound** [saʊnd] *adj.* 稳当的；安稳的
   William always offers sound financial advice.

行业之道 ｜ 品牌哲学 ｜ 财经内幕 ｜ 商海拾趣 ｜ 环球生活

CNN ANCHOR

As Kathleen Koch reports, it pulls no punches, even when it comes to the party he most closely identifies[5] with.

ALAN GREENSPAN, FED CHAIRMAN

The economy appeared to have considerable[6] momentum.[7]

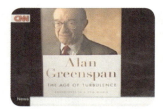

KATHLEEN KOCH, CNN CORRESPONDENT

While Chairman of the Federal Reserve, Alan Greenspan's words moved markets. Now in his new memoir, he's trading cautious,[8] cryptic[9] comments for blunt[10] criticism. And Washington is dissecting[11] his conclusions. One of Greenspan's most explosive charges, quote, "Everyone knows the Iraq war is largely about oil."

REP. TOM LANTOS (D), CALIFORNIA

It is very remarkable[12] that it took Alan Greenspan all these many years and being out of office for stating the obvious.

CNN 主播

凯瑟琳·柯赫的报道指出，这部回忆录毫无保留，即便涉及他自己的政党也不例外。

前美联储主席 艾伦·格林斯潘

目前经济增长似乎相当强劲。

CNN 特派员 凯瑟琳·柯赫

在前美联储主席任内，格林斯潘的话足以左右市场。现在，他在新出版的回忆录里，不再采取模棱两可的谨慎评论，而是改为直截了当的批判。华盛顿目前也正在分析他的结论。格林斯潘最具爆炸性的一项指控就是以下这句话：“所有人都知道伊拉克战争主要是为了石油。”

加州众议员（民主党）蓝托斯

值得注意的是，这么显而易见的事实，格林斯潘竟然等了这么多年，在离开了公职之后，才终于说出口来。

Notes & Vocabulary

pull no punches 直言；直截了当

punch 是“用拳猛击；重击”，而 **pull** 在这里则是指控制力道、打轻拳，因此 **pull no punches** 就是毫不保留地使劲攻击，常用来比喻直接说或做某事，类似于中文中的“直言不讳”、“单刀直入”。

Rhonda **pulled no punches** when critiquing her friend's sculpture.
朗达直言批评她朋友的雕塑。

5. **identify** [aɪ`dɛntə͵faɪ] *v.* 认同
Successful investors identify market trends.

6. **considerable** [kən`sɪdərəbļ]
adj. 相当大的
It took considerable effort to finish the project on time.

7. **momentum** [`momɛntəm]
n. 动力；冲劲；气势

8. **cautious** [`kɔʃəs]
adj. 小心的；谨慎的
Cautious analysts gave the stock a hold recommendation.

9. **cryptic** [`krɪptɪk] *adj.* 隐秘的
Jenny's cryptic phone message was difficult to decipher.

10. **blunt** [blʌnt]
adj. 直率的；直言不讳的
Wendy is always blunt when giving criticism to her friends.

11. **dissect** [dɪ`sɛkt] *v.* 仔细剖析
Alice dissected her boyfriend's poorly worded argument.

12. **remarkable** [rɪ`mɑrkəbļ]
adj. 非凡的；卓越的
Gina is remarkable for her singing ability.

行业之道 品牌哲学 财经内幕 商海拾趣 环球生活

ROBERT GATES, DEFENSE SECRETARY

I know the same allegation[13] was made about the Gulf War in 1991, and I just don't believe it's true.

KATHLEEN KOCH, CNN CORRESPONDENT

Greenspan blasts[14] President Bush for not vetoing[15] a single spending bill until nearly six years into his presidency. Quote, "Bush's collaborate[16]-don't-confront[17] approach[18] was a major mistake. 'Deficits[19] don't matter' to my chagrin became part of Republicans' rhetoric.[20]"

White House Deputy[21] Press Secretary Tony Fratto fired back. Quote, "We had veto threats which were used to good effect to keep spending within the president's numbers. Because Congress worked with us, vetoes weren't necessary."

国防部长 罗伯特·盖茨

我知道有人对 1991 年的海湾战争也提出过同样的指控，但我不相信这种说法。

CNN 特派员 凯瑟琳·柯赫

格林斯潘抨击布什总统在任的前 6 年间完全不曾否决过任何一项支出法案。他在书中是这么写的："布什采取合作而不对立的做法是一大错误。令我懊恼的是，'赤字没关系'竟然成了共和党习以为常的说辞。"

白宫副发言人汤尼·弗拉托提出反击。他说："我们有效否决了各种威胁，于是得以把支出控制在总统预期的范围内。由于国会和我们携手合作，因此也就不需要动用否决权。"

Notes & Vocabulary

to one's chagrin 让某人觉得羞愧

chagrin [ʃəˋgrin] 是"懊恼；悔恨；羞愧"的意思，源自法语，指因为失败、失望或丢脸的事而感到非常不舒服。to one's chagrin 表示对某人来说很可耻、可恼的意思。

· To Barbara's chagrin, Alex was late for dinner again.
艾力克斯晚餐又迟到了，芭芭拉对此很恼火。

13. **allegation** [ˌælɪˋgeʃən]
    n. 申述；主张

14. **blast** [blæst]
    v. 严词批评；强烈谴责
    Critics blasted the film's violence.

15. **veto** [ˋveto] *v. n.* 否决；否决权
    The president vetoed the legislation.

16. **collaborate** [kəˋlæbəret]
    v. 共同合作
    The two writers collaborated on a book.

17. **confront** [kənˋfrʌnt] *v.* 对抗
    Jack confronted his wife about her credit card bill.

18. **approach** [əˋprotʃ]
    n. 方法；取向

19. **deficit** [ˋdɛfəsət] *n.* 赤字

20. **rhetoric** [ˋrɛtərɪk] *n.* 辞令；说法

21. **deputy** [ˋdɛpjətɪ] *n.* 代理人；副手

行业之道 ― 品牌哲学 ― 财经内幕 ― 商海拾趣 ― 环球生活

Greenspan blames Republicans' lack of fiscal[22] discipline[23] for their 2006 loss of power in Congress, saying they, quote, "lost their way. They swapped[24] principle for power. They ended up with neither. They deserved to lose."

SEN. JOHN CORNYN (R), TEXAS
I agree that Republicans have unfortunately been guilty of too much spending in Washington, wasteful Washington spending, and we need to do better.

KATHLEEN KOCH, CNN CORRESPONDENT
In the book and in an interview on CBS's 60 Minutes, Greenspan defends his 2003 decision to keep short-term interest rates at one percent for a year, a move some say helped create the housing bubble that has now burst.

ALAN GREENSPAN, FED CHAIRMAN
It was our job to unfreeze the American banking system if we wanted the economy to function. This required that we keep rates modestly[25] low.

KATHLEEN KOCH, CNN CORRESPONDENT
Greenspan's criticism of President Bush and his party is particularly biting because it comes from a self-described libertarian[26] Republican. Still, Deputy Press Secretary Tony Fratto in a statement insists, quote, "at any rate, where we ended up on economic policy was right, as our records show."

格林斯潘把共和党在 2006 年丧失国会优势归咎于该党缺乏财政风纪。他说共和党"迷失了方向。他们放弃原则以换取权利，结果两头落空。败选是应该的。"

德州参议员（共和党）　孔宁

我同意，共和党执政时确实犯了过度支出以及浪费的错误。我们必须改正。

CNN 特派员　凯瑟琳·柯赫

格林斯潘在 2003 年决定把短期利率维持在 1% 达一年的时间。有些人认为此举促成了目前破灭的房市泡沫。格林斯潘不但在书中为这项决定提出辩护，在 CBS 电视台的《60 分钟》节目上接受专访的时候也重申了这一点。

前美联储主席　艾伦·格林斯潘

如果要让经济运作，我们就有责任为美国的银行体系解冻。要达到这个目的，就必须把利率压在低点。

CNN 特派员　凯瑟琳·柯赫

格林斯潘对布什总统以及共和党提出的批评特别尖锐，因为他自称是信奉自由放任主义的共和党人。不过，副发言人弗拉托在一份声明中仍旧坚称："无论如何，根据记录，我们的经济政策毕竟是正确的。"

Notes & Vocabulary

lose one's way
迷路；迷失
原本是"迷路；迷途；迷失方向"的意思，用来比喻做事或思考偏离方向，或彷徨迷惘、不知所措。

The film company lost its way after branching into the software industry.
那家电影公司在跨界软件业后就偏离了方向。

22. **fiscal** [ˈfɪskəl] *adj.* 财政的；国库的
Rhonda prepares her taxes at the end of every fiscal year.

23. **discipline** [ˈdɪsəplən]
n. 训练；纪律

24. **swap** [ˈswɑp] *v.* 以……作交换
Ben swapped his stocks for bonds.

25. **modestly** [ˈmɑdəstlɪ]
adv. 适度地；谨慎地

26. **libertarian** [lɪbəˈtɛrɪən]
adj. 自由开放派的
Nathan is libertarian in his political leanings.

行业之道　品牌哲学　财经内幕　商海拾趣　环球生活

Federal Reserve System 联邦储备制度

 又称为 Federal Reserve 或 The Fed ，指该单位时中文译为"联邦储备委员会"或简称"美联储"。

成立经过

目前的美联储是美国史上第三次建立的中央银行体系（central banking system），为独立的半官营（quasi-government）机构。20 世纪初美国国会成立国家货币委员会（National Monetary Commission），1913 年通过联邦储备法（Federal Reserve Act），1914 年开始实施。

主要部门

理事会 Board of Governors：共 7 人，由总统指派、经参议院同意，任期 14 年，由总统撤换。负责制定货币供给（monetary supply）政策、监督美联储运作及维持美国各银行稳定等。

公开市场委员会 Federal Open Market Committee：共 12 人，由理事会 7 人加上储备银行推荐的 5 人，其中纽约区为永久（permanent）委员，其他区每二至三年轮替。通过授权参与机构（authorized participant）在市场中买卖证券（securities），以控制利率及货币流通量。

联邦储备银行 Federal Reserve Banks：按区域结构划分为 12 个区，设置 12 个区域银行及 24 个分行。

私营会员银行 Private U.S. Member Banks：约 4800 家，拥有各区域储备银行的股份。

Alan Greenspan 艾伦·格林斯潘

出生

1926 年 3 月 6 日出生于纽约一个爱尔兰（Irish ）及德国犹太家庭

学历

1948　取得纽约大学经济学学士学位（B.S.）

1950　取得纽约大学经济学硕士学位（M.A.）

1977　获颁纽约大学经济学博士（Ph.D.）

2005　再获颁纽约大学商学（Commercial Science）荣誉博士（honorary doctor）

Erin Crowe 绘制 / TONGTONG 提供

经历

1948–1953　于纽约美国经济评议会（The Conference Board）担任经济分析研究员。

1954–1987　成立 Townsend-Greenspan Inc. 经济顾问公司，任董事长兼首席执行官。

1974–1977　被福特总统选中担任经济顾问委员会（Council of Economic Advisers）主席。

1987–2006　美联储主席，由里根总统任命后，历经老布什、克林顿及小布什共四位、五任总统，主导美国国内经济政策（domestic economic policy）长达20 年。

行业之道 | 品牌哲学 | 财经内幕 | 商海拾趣 | 环球生活

Bled Dry

Corrupt[1] Capitalism[2] Sends Mattress[3] Icon to Its Deathbed[4]

图片提供：美联储

ANDERSON COOPER, AC360

Tonight, I want to tell you about the death of an American company and a question: Is Wall Street's buyout[5] boom to blame? Last year, the Simmons Bedding Company laid off[6] a thousand employees, a full quarter of its workforce. It's about to declare bankruptcy now.

The recession[7] hasn't helped, but there's also this: Simmons has had a half dozen owners over the last two decades, and it's about to be sold again. That bankruptcy filing[8] is part of the deal.

So, who's behind the deal? Randi Kaye tonight is "Keeping Them Honest."

14-F.MP3
14-S.MP3

《360° 全面视野》安德森·古柏

今晚，我要和各位谈谈一家美国公司的衰亡，也要提出一个问题：华尔街的收购热潮是不是罪魁祸首？去年，席梦思床垫公司裁员一千人，比例高达全体员工的四分之一。现在，这家公司即将宣布破产。

经济衰退自然无助于这家公司的健全运作，但另外还有一个因素：席梦思在过去 20 年来已换手经营五六次，现在又要再次出售。破产申请正是这次交易的要求之一。

究竟这场交易的主导人是谁？今晚，兰迪·凯依要让他们"实话实说"。

Notes & Vocabulary

1. **corrupt** [kə`rʌpt]
   adj. 腐败的；贪污的
   The corrupt public official was sentenced to several years in prison.

2. **capitalism** [`kæpətəˌlɪsəm]
   n. 资本主义

3. **mattress** [`mætrəs] *n.* 床垫

4. **deathbed** [`dɛθˌbɛd]
   n. 临终床；临终之时

5. **buyout** [`baɪˌaut]
   n. 收购；买断

6. **lay off** [le] [ɔf] 遣散；解雇
   The company laid off half of its staff.

7. **recession** [rɪ`sɛʃən]
   n. 经济衰退；不景气

8. **filing** [`faɪlɪŋ] *n.* 诉请；申请；归档

RANDI KAYE, CNN CORRESPONDENT

It's what some call the dirty little secret of corporate takeovers[9]—private equity[10] firm buys undervalued[11] company using mostly borrowed money, then sells that company for a profit. At that point, the company is ruined, in some cases bankrupt. And, yes, it's all legal.

Forbes magazine columnist Dan Gerstein.

Should Americans be concerned about this?

DAN GERSTEIN, COLUMNIST, FORBES MAGAZINE

Every American should be losing sleep over this story because of what it says about how corrupt capitalism is.

RANDI KAYE, CNN CORRESPONDENT

Losing sleep over the story of Simmons Bedding Company, an American icon founded more than 130 years ago. Today, Simmons is on the verge of[12] bankruptcy.

Simmons' filings with the Securities & Exchange Commission show ever since the equity firm Thomas H. Lee Partners—or THL—bought Simmons in 2003, the bedding giant increased its debt by more than $700 million. Why? THL issued loans against Simmons, using the company's assets as collateral.[13] Even as Simmons was headed toward bankruptcy, THL pocketed $77 million.

How in the world does that happen? We had the same question.

CNN 特派员 兰迪·凯依

有些人称之为企业并购的龌龊小秘密——私营公司利用贷款买下价值遭到低估的公司，再转卖获利。这么一来，公司就毁了，甚至不免破产。而且，没错，这一切都是合法的。

我们采访到了《福布斯》杂志专栏作家丹·格斯坦。

美国人民应该对此感到关切吗？

《福布斯》杂志专栏作家 丹·格斯坦

每个美国人看到这则报道都应该晚上睡不着觉才对，因为这个新闻揭示了资本主义有多么腐败。

CNN 特派员 兰迪·凯依

我们应该为了席梦思床垫公司的新闻睡不着觉。这家公司早已成为美国公司的一个代表。它创立于 130 多年前，现在濒临破产边缘。

席梦思向美国证券交易委员会提出的申请显示，自从简称 THL 的资本运营公司汤玛斯·李集团在 2003 年买下席梦思之后，这家床垫大厂的负债就增加了超过 7 亿美元。为什么？因为 THL 贷款给席梦思，并以席梦思的资产作为担保。结果，就在席梦思走向破产的同时，THL 却赚进了 7700 万美元。

这种事情到底是怎么发生的？我们也有同样的疑问。

行业之道 | 品牌哲学 | 财经内幕 | 商海拾趣 | 环球生活

Notes & Vocabulary

9. **takeover** [ˈtekˌovɚ]
   n. 并购；占领；收购

10. **equity** [ˈɛkwətɪ]
    n. 公司股本；普通股；资产净值

11. **undervalued** [ˌʌndɚˈvæljud]
    adj. 估值不足的
    The investment analyst recommended buying undervalued stocks.

12. **on the verge of** 濒临；快要
    A treaty was signed just as the two countries were on the verge of going to war.

13. **collateral** [kəˈlætərəl]
    n. 担保品；抵押品

We came here to Boston, where Thomas H. Lee Partners is based, for some answers. Keeping them honest, we wanted the firm to tell us why Simmons racked up[14] so much debt under its watch and why the firm borrowed even more when Simmons was already strapped[15] for cash.

The firm would not give us an interview but did e-mail us a statement. THL says it added, quote, "sustainable and significant value to Simmons, including four new manufacturing facilities." The firm cited sales growth of 40 percent, but SEC filings paint a different picture.

We asked Maureen Spollen, an accountant with no connection to either THL or Simmons, to look at the financials.[16]

MAUREEN SPOLLEN, ACCOUNTANT, MIG CONSULTING
The year before they acquired[17] the company, it had $290 million worth of debt.

RANDI KAYE, CNN CORRESPONDENT
So that's 2002, and then in 2003, what did they have?

MAUREEN SPOLLEN, ACCOUNTANT, MIG CONSULTING
$770 million worth of debt. So it's more than double.

我们来到 THL 所在地波士顿寻找答案。我们要让这家公司实话实说，要求他们说明席梦思为何会在他们的经营下产生那么多债务，以及在席梦思早已严重缺钱的时候，他们为什么还会一再借钱。

这家公司不肯接受我们的采访，但以电子邮件寄来了一份声明。THL 表示自己"为席梦思增加了永续而且重要的资产，包括四座新的制造工厂"。他们称销量增长了 40%，但席梦思向美国证券交易委员会提出的申请书却呈现出不同的样子。

我们找了莫琳·史波兰，她是一位和 THL 或席梦思都没有关系的会计师。我们请她审视这两家公司的财务状况。

MIG 资产管理顾问公司会计师 莫琳·史波兰
在他们并购的前一年，这家公司就已经有 2.9 亿美元的债务。

CNN 特派员 兰迪·凯依
那是 2002 年了。2003 年的状况呢？

MIG 资产管理顾问公司会计师 莫琳·史波兰
7.7 亿美元的债务，增加幅度超过一倍。

14. **rack up** [ræk] [ʌp]
累积；累计；积聚
Jennifer racked up serious commissions from her latest sales.

15. **strapped** [stræpt]
adj. 缺钱的；手头紧的
Ron is strapped for cash, so he won't be going to Macau with us this weekend.

16. **financials** [fəˈnænʃəlz]
n. 财务数据、报表等（复数）

17. **acquire** [əˈkwaɪr] *v.* 购得；获得

RANDI KAYE, CNN CORRESPONDENT
And then if you jump ahead to, say, 2005?

MAUREEN SPOLLEN, ACCOUNTANT, MIG CONSULTING
It's over 900 million.

RANDI KAYE, CNN CORRESPONDENT
In debt?

MAUREEN SPOLLEN, ACCOUNTANT, MIG CONSULTING
In debt.

RANDI KAYE, CNN CORRESPONDENT
And then the end of this year?

MAUREEN SPOLLEN, ACCOUNTANT, MIG CONSULTING
It's over a billion.

RANDI KAYE, CNN CORRESPONDENT
So in the six years that THL has owned Simmons, the debt has, what, tripled?

MAUREEN SPOLLEN, ACCOUNTANT, MIG CONSULTING
It's tripled.

RANDI KAYE, CNN CORRESPONDENT
And all of this is legal?

Notes & Vocabulary

CNN 特派员 兰迪·凯依

如果再往后跳到，例如说，2005 年呢？

MIG 资产管理顾问公司会计师 莫琳·史波兰

超过 9 亿美元。

CNN 特派员 兰迪·凯依

负债吗？

MIG 资产管理顾问公司会计师 莫琳·史波兰

负债。

CNN 特派员 兰迪·凯依

这一年底呢？

MIG 资产管理顾问公司会计师 莫琳·史波兰

超过 10 亿。

CNN 特派员 兰迪·凯依

所以，在 THL 拥有席梦思的 6 年间，债务增长了 3 倍？

MIG 资产管理顾问公司会计师 莫琳·史波兰

没错，3 倍。

CNN 特派员 兰迪·凯依

这一切都是合法的？

行业之道

品牌哲学

财经内幕

商海拾趣

环球生活

MAUREEN SPOLLEN, ACCOUNTANT, MIG CONSULTING
Yes.

RANDI KAYE, CNN CORRESPONDENT
What isn't included on Simmons' balance sheet is a loan from 2007 for $300 million. The firm issued[18] this massive loan, creating even more debt for Simmons to pay out, just so THL could pay itself hundreds of millions of dollars in dividends.[19] Add that to earlier dividends, and THL recouped[20] all of its investment plus $77 million in profits.

DAN GERSTEIN, COLUMNIST, FORBES MAGAZINE
They were bleeding big chunks of that capital out and putting it in their pocket rather than having it go to the company. There isn't accountability,[21] and as a result, they get away with financial murder.

RANDI KAYE, CNN CORRESPONDENT
In a statement, THL suggests the economy is to blame for Simmons' financial mess, saying, quote, "The entire bedding industry was hit by an unprecedented,[22] cataclysmic[23] downturn."

Don't blame the economy, says Gerstein.

MIG 资产管理顾问公司会计师 莫琳·史波兰

没错。

CNN 特派员 兰迪·凯侬

有一项债务没有记载在席梦思的资产负债表上，那就是 2007 年借贷的 3 亿美元。THL 核发了这项庞大的贷款，给席梦思带来了更多的负债，为的是让 THL 能够付给自己数亿美元的红利。再加上以前的红利，即可发现 THL 不但全部的投资都回本了，还多赚 770 万美元的利润。

《福布斯》杂志专栏作家 丹·格斯坦

他们从那笔资金中榨了大笔钱财，放进自己的口袋里，而不是交给席梦思。我们不能追究他们的责任，所以他们虽然犯下了财务谋杀的罪行，却还是能够全身而退。

CNN 特派员 兰迪·凯侬

在一份声明里，THL 宣称席梦思的财务窘境必须归咎于经济大环境。其中指出："整个床垫产业都遭到史无前例的重大衰退与冲击。"

别怪罪经济状况，格斯坦说。

---

⑭ 美国资本市场的警钟——席梦思破产内幕

Notes & Vocabulary

bleed...out 榨光……的钱

bleed 当及物动词时指"使流血；吸血；抽取汁液"，引申为"榨取钱财；勒索"，类似于中文用"失血"来比喻金钱损失。**bleed ...out** 表示"榨光……的钱财"，和标题 **bleed sb. dry** 意思相似。

· The new owners **bled** the company **out** by selling off its assets.
新的老板抛售了这家公司的资产，从中榨取利润。

· Credit card debt has **bled** Nancy **dry**.
信用卡债榨干了南希的钱。

18. **issue** [ˈɪʃu] *v.* 发给；供给
The company issued loans against its property holdings.

19. **dividend** [ˈdɪvəˌdɛnd]
n. 红利；股息

20. **recoup** [rɪˈkup] *v.* 补偿；偿还
Few investors recouped their losses after the stock market crashed.

21. **accountability** [əˌkaʊntəˈbɪlətɪ]
n. 有责任

22. **unprecedented** [ʌnˈprɛsəˌdɛntəd]
adj. 空前的；前所未有的；史无前例的
Jenny issued an unprecedented apology at the meeting.

23. **cataclysmic** [ˌkætəˈklɪzmɪk]
adj. 剧变的；灾难性的
A cataclysmic explosion leveled the building.

行业之道　品牌哲学　财经内幕　商海拾趣　环球生活

DAN GERSTEIN, COLUMNIST, FORBES MAGAZINE
It's because they were so loaded up with debt, they didn't have the means to weather the storm, and it's a good, you know, indictment[24] and a cautionary[25] tale for what's wrong with our economy. They were doing something that was pretty common in the industry.

RANDI KAYE, CNN CORRESPONDENT
Standard, maybe. Risk free? Definitely not.

Simmons Bedding Company 席梦思创始大事记

1870	札尔曼·席梦思先生（Zalmon G. Simmons）于威斯康新州克诺沙市设立第一家工厂，生产木质绝缘体（insulator）及奶酪盒。
1876	运用手工编织弹簧的技术，开始生产弹簧床。
1925	发明量产（mass-produce）独立筒弹簧圈（coil）的机器。
1975	总部迁到现址佐治亚州亚特兰大市（Atlanta, Georgia）。
1979	被 Gulf+Western 制造集团收购。
1985	被卖给零售公司 Wickes Corporation。
1986	被投资公司 Wesray Capital 及席梦思许多高层主管买下。
1991	美林证券 Merrill Lynch Capital Partners 买下 60% 股权并承担负债。
1996	美林将持股卖给巴林投资集团 Investcorp。
1998	Investcorp 将持股卖给投资公司 Fenway Partner。
2003	私营公司 Thomas H. Lee Partners 买下席梦思。
2006	席梦思将旗下连锁店卖给床垫零售商 The Sleep Train。
2009	申请破产并由私募基金 Ares Management 和安大略教师退休金计划（Ontario Teachers' Pension Plan）收购。

《福布斯》杂志专栏作家 丹·格斯坦

因为他们的负债太沉重了，才会没有办法渡过难关。这样的结果不但是一项鲜明的指控，也是一则警世寓言。它显示了我们经济的问题究竟出在哪里。他们的所作所为在业界是相当常见的现象。

CNN 特派员 兰迪·凯依

典型做法，也许。零风险吗？绝对不是。

Notes & Vocabulary

weather the storm
渡过难关
weather 当动词时指"经受住；坚韧地渡过"，**weather the storm** 字面上是"渡过暴风雨"，用来比喻"坚持着渡过难关"。

The economic crisis has been difficult for many businesses, but the stronger ones should weather the storm.
经济危机让许多公司很艰难，但强健者应该能渡过难关。

24. **indictment** [ɪnˋdaɪtmənt]
    n.（制度、社会等的）腐败迹象；控告；起诉

25. **cautionary** [ˋkɔʃənerɪ]
    adj. 警告的；劝告的
    The story was a cautionary tale about the importance of honesty.

行业之道 | 品牌哲学 | 财经内幕 | 商海拾趣 | 环球生活

Savior[1] or Saboteur[2]?

Did Alan Greenspan's Own Policies Build and Then Burst the Housing Bubble?

图片提供：Reuters

ANDY SERWER, MANAGING EDITOR, FORTUNE

For nearly two decades, the throne[3] at the Federal Reserve was occupied by one man, Chairman Alan Greenspan. The so-called maestro[4] fattened America's piggy bank[5] during the dot-com '90s, overseeing the biggest economic boom in modern times.

Two Clinton administration treasury secretaries[6] shared the cover of *Time* magazine with Greenspan. It was titled "Committee to Save the World." Larry Summers remembers the Clinton White House was itching[7] to take credit for[8] the good times.

15-F.MP3
15-S.MP3

《财富》执行总编辑 安迪·索尔

在将近 20 年的时间里，美联储的宝座被一个人独占着，他就是艾伦·格林斯潘。这个人们口中的大师在属于网络公司的 20 世纪 90 年代里大大地充实了美国国库，并负责督导了近代史上最大规模的经济增长。

两任克林顿政府的财政部长和格林斯潘一同登上过《时代》杂志的封面，标题为"拯救世界的委员会"。赖瑞·桑默斯回忆，克林顿的白宫幕僚团迫不及待地想将经济繁荣的功劳往身上揽。

Notes & Vocabulary

1. **savior** [ˋsevjə] *n.* 救星；救难者

2. **saboteur** [ˌsæbəˋtɜ]
   n. 搞阴谋破坏者

3. **throne** [θron]
   n. 宝座；王位；王权

4. **maestro** [ˋmaɪstro]
   n. 大师；名家

5. **piggy bank** [ˋpɪgɪ] [bænk]
   猪形存钱罐；存钱筒

6. **treasury secretary**
   [ˋtrɛʒərɪ] [ˋsɛkrəˌtɛrɪ] 财政部长

7. **itch** [ɪtʃ] *v.* 渴望；极想
   Chet is itching to go back to school and earn his master's degree.

8. **take credit for** 邀功
   Alan took credit for his department's boost in sales.

行业之道 品牌哲学 财经内幕 商海拾趣 环球生活

LARRY SUMMERS, FORMER U.S TREASURY SECRETARY
People in the White House were always suggesting that the president or the secretary of the Treasury, or other senior officials go to the White House and celebrate how high the stock market prices were. I advised the president and advised others that "live by the sword, die by the sword," it was a mistake to do photo ops[9] that were based on the level of markets.

ANDY SERWER, MANAGING EDITOR, FORTUNE
They took his advice. Neither President Clinton nor Alan Greenspan ever rang the opening bell. But when Greenspan left office in 2006, no one sounded any alarm bells, either. The overheated economy was about to boil over. Suddenly, Greenspan found himself on the defensive.

ALAN GREENSPAN, FORMER CH., U.S. FEDERAL RESERVE
This was an accident waiting to happen. If it weren't subprime, it would have been something else.

ANDY SERWER, MANAGING EDITOR, FORTUNE
In *Greenspan's Bubbles*, author and investor Bill Fleckenstein takes a critical look at Greenspan's tenure.[10]

美国前财政部长 赖瑞·桑默斯

白宫的人当时老是建议总统、财政部长或其他资深官员到白宫来庆祝一下股价有多高。我建议总统和其他人说："水能载舟，也能覆舟"，基于股市行情高而拍照宣传是不对的。

《财富》执行总编辑 安迪·索尔

他们采纳了他的意见。无论克林顿总统还是格林斯潘都未曾去敲开市钟。但是当格林斯潘在 2006 年退休时，也没有任何人敲过警钟。过热的经济已经要沸腾了。忽然间，格林斯潘发现要开始为自己辩护了。

前美联储主席 艾伦·格林斯潘

这场意外迟早会发生。就算不是次级房贷，也会是别的事情。

《财富》执行总编辑 安迪·索尔

在《格林斯潘的泡沫》一书中，作者兼投资人比尔·佛列克斯坦对于格林斯潘在任期中的作为多有批判。

---

⑮ 美国房市泡沫化，格林斯潘是罪魁祸首?

live by the sword, die by the sword

出自《新约》马太福音，耶稣让门徒把剑收起来，原文为 "all who draw the sword will die by the sword" "凡动刀的，必死在刀下"。原本是比喻 "行恶者必自受其害"，类似于中文的 "玩火者必自焚"。后来较常用的说法为 live by the sword, die by the sword，表示对某事 "蒙其利，受其害"，类似于成语中的 "水能载舟，也能覆舟" 或 "成也萧何，败也萧何"。

on the defensive
采取守势

defensive 当名词时指 "防御；守势；防守状态"，on the defensive 表示遭到攻击或批评时，必须或准备采取防守、捍卫的状态。

·Jim was on the defensive when his manager accused him of a lapse in productivity.
吉姆在经理指责他害得产量下滑时捍卫自己。

9. photo op [ˈfoto] [ɑp]
（名人、政要）媒体拍照时间

10. tenure [ˈtɛnjɚ] *n.* 任期

行业之道 | 品牌哲学 | 财经内幕 | 商海拾趣 | 环球生活

BILL FLECKENSTEIN, AUTHOR AND INVESTOR

In an attempt to fight off the ill effects of the stock bubble, we wound up with a real estate bubble. One of the consequences of Greenspan's reign[11] at the Fed is we in America have sort of bastardized[12] capitalism in that we don't ever seem to want to have the downside of it anymore. We want the upside and then more upside, and that's not how it works.

ANDY SERWER, MANAGING EDITOR, FORTUNE

To be fair, Greenspan did warn us of the dot-com bubble back in 1996, in his trademark Fed-speak.

ALAN GREENSPAN, FORMER CH., U.S. FEDERAL RESERVE

But how do we know when irrational exuberance[13] has unduly[14] escalated[15] asset values?

⑮ 美国房市泡沫化，格林斯潘是罪魁祸首？

作者兼投资人 比尔·佛列克斯坦

为了试图对抗股市泡沫化带来的不良后果，我们到头来却造了一个房地产大泡沫。格林斯潘担任美联储主席期间造成的后果之一是，我们在美国的人拥有一种趋于低劣的资本主义思想，因此我们似乎不想再经历任何经济衰退了。我们要的是经济繁荣，然后更多的繁荣，但经济不是这样运作的。

《财富》执行总编辑 安迪·索尔

客观地说，格林斯潘确实早在 1996 年时便对我们提出过网络泡沫的警告，用的是他那招牌式的美联储说辞。

前美联储主席 艾伦·格林斯潘

但我们如何知道不理性的繁荣在何时已经过度地抬高了资产价值呢？

Notes & Vocabulary

wind up with 结果；最后

wind up 是指"使某事结束"或"整理并做总结"，例如 wind up the meeting。文中为不及物动词的用法，表示"结果变成……"的意思，后面用 with 加上所得到的后果。也可用 end up with。

· After years of careful investing, Betty ended up with a small fortune.

经过多年的小心投资，贝蒂最后发了一笔小财。

to be fair 客观地说

fair 当形容词有"公平；公正"的意思，to be fair 是指"公平地说"，放在发表意见或阐述某事之前，表示认为这样说是公正的。

· Matt might not be the best player at the tennis club, but to be fair, he is the oldest.

麦特也许不是网球俱乐部里最厉害的选手，但公平地说，他是最资深的。

11. **reign** [ren] *n.* 统治；在位期间

12. **bastardized** [ˈbæstɚˌdaɪzd] *adj.* 非正宗的；伪劣的
California cuisine is a bastardized fusion of regional cooking traditions that focuses on fresh local ingredients.

13. **exuberance** [ɪgˈzubərəns] *n.* 繁茂；蓬勃

14. **unduly** [ˌʌnˈdjulɪ] *adv.* 过度地；过分地

15. **escalate** [ˈɛskəlet] *v.* 逐步上升、扩大
The military confrontation escalated after the attempted assassination of the president.

行业之道 品牌哲学 财经内幕 商海拾趣 环球生活

141

ANDY SERWER, MANAGING EDITOR, FORTUNE

Irrational exuberance: Greenspan's subtle[16] warning conceived in a bathtub, now part of Wall Street lexicon.[17] I sat down with Greenspan just as the housing bubble was bursting.

ALAN GREENSPAN, FORMER CH., U.S. FEDERAL RESERVE

We have been through this type of event innumerable times over the centuries. We get to a state of extraordinary exuberance, which, when confronted with reality, turns to unrelenting[18] fear.

ANDY SERWER, MANAGING EDITOR, FORTUNE

But how could he have not seen this housing bubble coming? After all, his public service spanned six presidencies, four of which he served as Fed chairman.

ALAN GREENSPAN, FORMER CH., U.S. FEDERAL RESERVE

Thank you very much.

ANDY SERWER, MANAGING EDITOR, FORTUNE

Greenspan first took the title of Mr. Chairman in 1987. Ten weeks into the job, stocks plunged[19] 508 points, the biggest one-day loss ever. The *New York Times* headline read, "Does 1987 equal 1929?" But within 15 months, the market would recover all of its losses and was roaring again. That's why this real estate bust,[20] according to Greenspan, is just another giant market correction.

Greenspan's critics say he failed to step in, or, as a former Fed chairman once said, it's the Fed's role to take away the punch bowl when the party's warming up.

《财富》执行总编辑 安迪·索尔

不理性的繁荣：这个格林斯潘在泡澡时想出来的隐语似的警告，现在已被收入华尔街的辞典中了。我在房市泡沫正要破裂时采访了格林斯潘。

前美联储主席 艾伦·格林斯潘

过去几个世纪以来，我们已经经历过无数次这一类的事件了。我们处在一个无比繁荣的景况中，然而一旦我们面对现实的时候，这又变成了无情的恐惧。

《财富》执行总编辑 安迪·索尔

但他为何没能事先看到房市泡沫的降临呢？毕竟他的公职生涯跨越了 6 任总统，其中有 4 任是由他担任美联储主席的。

前美联储主席 艾伦·格林斯潘

非常感谢你。

《财富》执行总编辑 安迪·索尔

格林斯潘最早是在 1987 年就任美联储主席的。刚上任十周后，股市便重挫了 508 点，创下史上单日最大跌幅。《纽约时报》的标题写道："1987 年等于 1929 年吗？"但是 15 个月内，股市便收复所有损失，再次大涨。这也就是为什么这次房市重挫，根据格林斯潘的说法，只不过是又一次的市场大幅修正罢了。

批评格林斯潘的人说，格林斯潘错在没有介入，或是诚如一位前美联储主席所言，美联储所扮演的角色就是在派对气氛热起来的时候把鸡尾酒缸收走。

Notes & Vocabulary

step in

介入；干预

step in 原本是指"跨进；踏入"一个空间，引申为"介入；干预"某事物，阻挠或影响其发展的过程。

· The large automaker stepped in to buy out a struggling competitor.

那家汽车制造大厂介入收购了一个生存困难的对手。

16. subtle [ˈsʌtl] *adj.* 微微的；隐约的
Ralph tasted a subtle hint of fennel in the pasta dish.

17. lexicon [ˈlɛksəˌkɑn] *n.* 词汇

18. unrelenting [ˌʌnrɪˈlɛntɪŋ]
adj. 无情的；坚定的
The police were unrelenting in their pursuit of the killer.

19. plunge [plʌndʒ] *v.* 急降；猛跌
The value of many houses plunged after the mortgage crisis.

20. bust [bʌst] *n.* 失败；破产

行业之道 | 品牌哲学 | 财经内幕 | 商海拾趣 | 环球生活

BILL FLECKENSTEIN, AUTHOR AND INVESTOR

The hangover[21] is going to have some correlation[22] to the size of the party. So the sooner you get on it the better. The Fed could have done many things. They could have used their bully pulpit to jawbone[23] about speculation.[24]

ANDY SERWER, MANAGING EDITOR, FORTUNE

Instead, in 2004, Greenspan used the bully pulpit to extol[25] the virtues of mortgage innovation.

ALAN GREENSPAN, FORMER CH., U.S. FEDERAL RESERVE

American consumers might benefit if lenders provided greater mortgage product alternatives to the traditional fixed-rate mortgage.

ANDY SERWER, MANAGING EDITOR, FORTUNE

Now, of course, people are pointing fingers at you, Chairman Greenspan, in terms of the so-called housing bubble bursting and saying that you're responsible or partly responsible. "Look at what he said in 2004: 'Adjustable-rate mortgages are prudent.[26]'" How do you respond to those critics?

作者兼投资人 比尔·佛列克斯坦

宿醉昏头的程度和派对的规模是有关系的，所以你越早介入越好。美联储原本可以做很多事的，他们原本可以用他们的绝佳讲坛来影响各方的臆测。

《财富》执行总编辑 安迪·索尔

格林斯潘反而还在 2004 年时通过美联储的绝佳讲坛赞扬房贷创新的好处。

前美联储主席 艾伦·格林斯潘

如果贷方提供比传统固定利率房贷更多的房贷产品让人们选择的话，那么美国消费者可能会因此而受惠。

《财富》执行总编辑 安迪·索尔

当然，现在大家都将矛头指向主席您本人，针对所谓房市泡沫的破灭，他们说您要负责任，或负部分责任，譬如有人说："你看他在 2004 年说过'可调整利率房贷是明智的。'"您如何回应这些批评呢？

Notes & Vocabulary

bully pulpit
绝佳讲坛；有利的发声位置

bully pulpit [ˈbʊlɪ] [ˈpʊlpɪt] 是比喻"有利于下达意见的高层职位"，尤其指政府要职，最早由美国前总统罗斯福用来描述总统职位。当时 bully 是"绝佳的；极好的"的意思，而非现在的"霸道；欺侮"。pulpit 是"讲坛"。

· The popular television host used his bully pulpit to champion the cause of the homeless.
那位人气电视主持人利用他有利的位置来帮助无家可归的人。

point fingers at sb. 指责某人

是骂人时指着对方的动作，故引申为"指责某人；责怪某人"，亦可写成 point the finger at。

· Many commentators have pointed fingers at the president's policies for the state of the economy.
许多评论家针对该国经济对总统提出指责。

21. **hangover** [ˈhæŋˌovə]
    n. 宿醉；残余物

22. **correlation** [ˌkɔrəˈleʃən]
    n. 相互关系；关联

23. **jawbone** [ˈdʒɔˌbon]
    v. 强力促使 n. 颌骨
    The car dealer jawboned Mark into buying an expensive SUV.

24. **speculation** [ˌspɛkjəˈleʃən]
    n. 臆测；推测

25. **extol** [ɪkˈstol] v. 赞扬；颂扬
    Drew extolled the virtues of his new all-fruit diet.

26. **prudent** [ˈprudənt]
    adj. 谨慎的；精明的

行业之道 | 品牌哲学 | 财经内幕 | 商海拾趣 | 环球生活

ALAN GREENSPAN, FORMER CH., U.S. FEDERAL RESERVE
I think revisionist[27] history is coming on with a rush. I thought that people who had special individual cases ought to be looking at adjustable-rate mortgages.

ANDY SERWER, MANAGING EDITOR, FORTUNE
But adjustable rate mortgages became the loan of choice[28] for subprime America, or those with poor credit histories.

ALAN GREENSPAN, FORMER CH., U.S. FEDERAL RESERVE
I don't know where you draw the line because a lot of the subprime lending has been, frankly, truly egregious[29] and, I think in many cases, criminal fraud.[30]

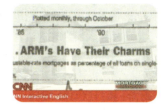

ANDY SERWER, MANAGING EDITOR, FORTUNE
But can a Fed chairman really save us from ourselves?

ALAN GREENSPAN, FORMER CH., U.S. FEDERAL RESERVE
The crucial issue of regulation is not to determine what people do, but create a system, which no matter what they do, it doesn't do significant harm to the economy.

ANDY SERWER, MANAGING EDITOR, FORTUNE
And by the way, guess who didn't get an adjustable rate mortgage.

ALAN GREENSPAN, FORMER CH., U.S. FEDERAL RESERVE
I like 30-year mortgages.

15-F.MP3 / 15-S.MP3 ❙ *Savior or Saboteur?*

前美联储主席 艾伦·格林斯潘

我认为修正派历史正急着想要出头。我当时认为那些拥有特殊情况的个人应该选择可调整型房贷。

《财富》执行总编辑 安迪·索尔

但是可调整型房贷成了美国次级信用人士，或是那些信用记录差的人特选的房贷。

前美联储主席 艾伦·格林斯潘

我不知道你是如何区分的，因为很多次级放款，老实说，真的很离谱，我认为有许多是犯罪欺诈。

《财富》执行总编辑 安迪·索尔

但是靠一位美联储主席真的就能拯救我们吗？

前美联储主席 艾伦·格林斯潘

法规真正的重点，不在于规定人们的行为，而是建立一套系统，让人们无论做了什么事，都不会对经济造成重大的伤害。

《财富》执行总编辑 安迪·索尔

顺便一提，猜猜看谁没有采用可调整型房贷？

前美联储主席 艾伦·格林斯潘

我喜欢 30 年期的（固定利率）房贷。

Notes & Vocabulary

draw the line 区别

字面意思是指"划分界线"，表示"将某物与另一物区别开来"，后面常用 at 表示"到······为止"。

· David may be low on cash, but he draws the line at borrowing money to make ends meet.
大卫也许缺钱，但他不会去借钱来支付开销。

27. **revisionist** [rɪˈvɪʒənɪst]
    adj. 修正主义的
    The revisionist historian's new book challenges many commonly held beliefs.

28. **of choice** [əv] [ˈtʃɔɪs]
    精选的；特别的
    Hybrids are the cars of choice for many environmentally conscious drivers.

29. **egregious** [ɪˈgridʒəs]
    adj. 岂有此理的；极糟的
    Not installing antivirus software on your computer is an egregious error.

30. **fraud** [frɔd] *n.* 诈欺；诈骗

行业之道 | 品牌哲学 | 财经内幕 | 商海拾趣 | 环球生活

商海拾趣

Gates on Giving

Microsoft Founder Discusses the Importance of Philanthropy[1] in Tough Times

图片提供：© 2008 Microsoft Corporation

FAREED ZAKARIA, GPS

We're all worried about the economy, and who better to ask about it than the richest man in the world. Bill Gates has occupied[2] that spot, with a few dips[3] here and there, since he was 37 years old. He's now 53, and we spoke about his extraordinary charitable[4] work, the future of technology, but also about his view of the American economy. The headline:[5] he's not too worried.

Are we, right now, in a kind of crisis of capitalism,[6] when you see the financial industry seeming to be in meltdown,[7] or in at least dramatic[8] reorganization? Is this the end of a certain kind of model of capitalism?

Notes & Vocabulary

16-F.MP3
16-S.MP3

名人小档案▼ 比尔·盖茨

全名：William Henry Bill Gates III

出生：1955 年 10 月 28 日生于西雅图

现任：微软公司董事长、比尔与梅琳
达·盖茨基金会联合主席

身价：580 亿美元（2008）

重要大事：

1975 年哈佛大学大三时辍学创办微软
公司

1985 年推出第一套微软操作系统

1994 年与妻子梅琳达·法兰奇结婚

1995 年成为《福布斯》全球首富（至
2008 年退居第三，由沃伦·巴
菲特拿下第一）

2008 年 6 月 27 日正式卸下微软公司
首席执行官等日常职务

《全球公共广场》法瑞德·札卡利亚

我们都对经济感到很忧心，关于这一点，有
谁比世界首富更适合成为我们请教的对象
呢？比尔·盖茨 37 岁当上世界首富，偶尔
有些起起落落。他今年 53 岁，我们谈到他
了不起的慈善工作，科技的未来，以及他对
于美国经济的看法。标题是：他不太担心。

我们现在是否置身于某种资本主义的危机
中？我们看到金融业似乎濒临瓦解，或者至
少在经历大幅重整，这是否是某种资本主义
模式的末路呢？

1. **philanthropy** [fəˈlænθrəpɪ]
   n. 慈善

2. **occupy** [ˈɑkjəˌpaɪ]
   v. 位居（某地位）；担任（职务）
   The movie occupied the top spot at
   the box office for several weeks.

3. **dip** [dɪp] *n.*（短暂）下跌；下降

4. **charitable** [ˈtʃærətəbl]
   adj. 慈善的；仁慈的
   Jenny gives a small percentage of her
   monthly salary to charitable
   organizations.

5. **headline** [ˈhɛdˌlaɪn]
   n. 大标题；头条消息

6. **capitalism** [ˈkæpətəˌlɪzm]
   n. 资本主义

7. **meltdown** [ˈmɛltˌdaʊn]
   n. 熔解；瓦解

8. **dramatic** [drəˈmætɪk]
   adj. 戏剧性的
   Bill made dramatic spending cuts to
   balance his budget.

行业之道

品牌哲学

财经内幕

商海拾趣

环球生活

BILL GATES, PHILANTHROPIST AND CO-FOUNDER OF MICROSOFT

No. Not at all.

It's a very interesting crisis, and it's important [that it ...] that things move forward, that markets are continuing to operate. And there's some type of correction we'll have to look at in terms of the leverage[9] we allow, the complexity[10] of balance sheets[11] we allow—people who are so key that the government feels like they have to come in and bail them out.

And there's a lot, a lot of thinking that has to go on, but fundamentally,[12] the total market valuation[13] of companies, companies' willingness to invest, right now we haven't seen a huge disruption[14] in that.

There may be ... it looks like the economy may be go down somewhat, but nothing like a big recession[15] or a depression.[16] And, you know, the amount of innovation[17] taking place, the amount of investment is actually greater today than ever, because you not only have more American companies with more scientists and engineers and innovators, but now you have what Friedman calls "the Flat World," where you have people from all over, including lots of people in India and China, now contributing to new drug design, new software design, new energy generation design.

慈善家及微软共同创办人　比尔·盖茨
不是，完全不是。

这是一场很令人玩味的危机，重要的是事情要继续往前进展，市场还要继续运作。我们应该从几个方面来看待经济修正，例如我们能容许的杠杆力量和资产负债表的复杂程度等等——有些人重要到政府觉得必须介入并协助其脱困。

要考虑的还有很多，但基本上，此刻我们并没有看到公司的整体市值和公司的投资意愿受到很大的破坏。

也许会有……看来经济可能会略微下挫，但是不会像大衰退或大萧条那么惨。还有，现在的创意规模和投资规模事实上要比以往任何时刻都大得多，因为不只有美国公司的科学家、工程师和发明家人数增加了，现在的世界一如佛里曼所言是个"扁平的世界"（注），来自世界各地的人，包括很多来自印度和中国的人，现在都在对发明新药、设计新软件和规划生产新能源等方面做出贡献。

注：汤马斯·佛里曼在畅销书《世界是平的：一部 21 世纪简史》（ *The World Is Flat: A Brief History of the Twenty-first Century* ）中提出，21 世纪初期，个人与企业通过全球化过程得到权力，使强权的经济竞争优势逐渐消失，"世界正被抹平（ flattening ）"。

Notes & Vocabulary

bail out 帮助某人（财务）脱困

bail out 原本是"保释某人"的意思，又比喻"协助某人摆脱困境"，尤其指财务方面。**bail** 本身当名词"保释金；保释判决"。

- The government bailed out the failed bank.
  政府援助那家破产的银行脱困。

补充

on bail 交保获释

- The suspect was released on bail pending his trial.
  该名嫌疑犯交保获释等候审理。

bailout *n.* 紧急财务援助；金融脱困

---

9. **leverage** [ˈlɛvərɪdʒ]
   n. 抗衡的影响力；杠杆作用

10. **complexity** [kəmˈplɛksətɪ]
    n. 复杂性

11. **balance sheet** [ˈbæləns] [ʃit]
    资产负债表

12. **fundamentally** [ˌfʌndəˈmɛntlɪ]
    adv. 基本上

13. **valuation** [ˌvæljəˈeʃən]
    n. 估定的价值；评估

14. **disruption** [dɪsˈrʌpʃən]
    n. 崩溃；瓦解

15. **recession** [rɪˈsɛʃən]
    n. （经济）衰退

16. **depression** [dɪˈprɛʃən]
    n. （经济）萧条；不景气

17. **innovation** [ˌɪnəˈveʃən]
    n. 创新；革新

行业之道　品牌哲学　财经内幕　商海拾趣　环球生活

FAREED ZAKARIA, GPS

You're gonna give away almost all your money. You're gonna give away almost all of Warren Buffett's money. That's, collectively, tens of billions of dollars. You've chosen something very unusual. Ninety-eight percent of the philanthropists[18] in the United States give the money in America, essentially to Americans. You chose not to do that. Why?

BILL GATES, PHILANTHROPIST AND CO-FOUNDER OF MICROSOFT

If you look and say, "Where is the greatest inequity[19]?" you have to take a global view of that. I mean, America stands for a lot of things. It stands for the innovation that a capitalistic society can drive.[20] It stands for political freedom.

But it also stands for ending inequity and over the decades, the inequities against women, or various religions, or races, America's made a lot of progress. And so, I think we can say today that the global economic inequity is the greatest one left and probably the hardest one to make progress on.

And so, the capitalistic approaches,[21] scientific innovation, decent[22] governance[23] —those things have been proven out in most of the world, and we should want to help the countries that have got

《全球公共广场》法瑞德·札卡利亚

您将捐出几乎您所有的钱财。您也将捐出几乎沃伦·巴菲特所有的钱财。这样加起来有数百亿美元之多。您做了极不寻常的选择。美国境内 98% 的慈善家在美洲将钱捐出，尤其是捐给美国人。您却选择不这么做，为什么？

慈善家及微软共同创办人　比尔·盖茨

如果你看看四周然后问："最不公平的地方在哪里？"那需要从全世界的角度来看。我的意思是，美国代表了很多东西。它支持一个资本主义社会可以带动出来的创新想法。它支持政治自由。

但它也支持终结不公平，而过去 10 年间，在对女性的不平等，或对各种宗教、种族面临的不平等方面，美国都有长足的进步。所以今天我们可以说全球经济的不公平现象，是最大的一种不公平，而且可能是最难取得进展的一种。

所以，资本运作的方式、科学创新、正派的管理，这些东西已经在世界绝大部分地区

Notes & Vocabulary

stand for 支持；代表

stand for 在文中是"支持"某种原则、理念的意思，另外还可指某事物"代表……意义"。

- The candidate's campaign stands for improving education.
  该候选人在竞选中支持教育发展。
- The stars on the U.S. flag stand for the 50 states.
  美国国旗上的星星代表该国的 50 个州。

其他与 stand 连用的词组

take a stand 表明立场

- Janice took a stand on literacy by donating money to her local library.
  珍尼丝捐款给当地的图书馆，表明支持推广阅读识字的立场。

stand tall 坚毅不屈；有自信的样子

- Dina stood tall in the face of personal tragedy when her husband was diagnosed with cancer.
  迪娜的丈夫被诊断出癌症，她用坚毅的态度面对这件个人灾难。

18. **philanthropist** [fə`lænθrəpɪst]
    n. 慈善家

19. **inequity** [ɪ`nɛkwətɪ]
    n. 不公平

20. **drive** [draɪv] *v.* 驱策；驱动
    Technology drives many Asian economies.

21. **approach** [ə`protʃ]
    n. 解决方法；态度

22. **decent** [dɪ`sɳt]
    adj. 正派的；像样的
    Mandy strives to lead a decent life.

23. **governance** [`gʌvənəns]
    n. 管理；统治

行业之道　品牌哲学　财经内幕　商海拾趣　环球生活

tough situations, to help them get on that same track.

FAREED ZAKARIA, GPS

Do you think history will remember you as the man who created Microsoft, or the man who created the Gates Foundation?

BILL GATES, PHILANTHROPIST AND CO-FOUNDER OF MICROSOFT

I, you know, who knows how history will think of me? As, you know, the person who played bridge with Warren Buffett, maybe. Or maybe not at all.

You know, most of the things we do, we do because of the people we care about, our family, because we love doing them every day. And, you know, it doesn't require a historical perspective.[24] You have values. You have things you enjoy, things you're good at, and for me, these foundation issues really fit every one of those characteristics.

The Bill & Melinda Gates Foundation
比尔与梅琳达盖茨基金会（B&MGF）

总部（headquarters）：西雅图

首席执行官（CEO）：杰夫 · 瑞克斯（Jeff Raikes）

共同主席（co-chairs）：盖茨夫妇与父亲威廉 · 盖茨

托管人（trustees）：盖茨夫妇与沃伦 · 巴菲特

拥有捐款（endowment）：387 亿美元

行善方式：捐款（donations）及资助（grants）申请

图片提供：Bill & Melinda Gates Foundation

16-F.MP3 / 16-S.MP3 | *Gates on Giving*

获得验证，我们应该要去帮助那些形势艰难的国家，帮助他们走上同样的道路。

《全球公共广场》法瑞德·札卡利亚

您认为历史会记住您是微软的创始者，还是盖茨基金会的创立者？

慈善家及微软共同创办人 比尔·盖茨

谁知道历史会怎么去认定我这个人。也许记得我是那个和沃伦·巴菲特打桥牌的家伙，或者什么都不是。

我们做的大部分事情，都是为了我们所关心的人、我们的家人，因为我们喜爱每天去做这些事。这并不需要有个历史观点。你会有价值观念。你有自己喜欢的事和自己拿手的事，对我而言，这些基金会的事务着实符合上述每一种特点。

主要目标：

全球——提高医疗（healthcare）条件、
　　　　终结赤贫
美国——增加就学机会、普及信息科技

发展计划：

全球健康（Global Health Program）
全球发展（Global Development Program）
全美事务（United States Program）

Notes & Vocabulary

on track
顺利进行

track 是指"轨道；路径；铁轨"等，on track 表示如预期或计划中那样"顺利进行"，如同顺着轨道走一般。

· Ben is on track to get into a top university.
班顺利朝着就读顶尖大学迈进。

24. **perspective** [pəˈspɛktɪv]
n. 看法；观点

行业之道 ｜ 品牌哲学 ｜ 财经内幕 ｜ 商海拾趣 ｜ 环球生活

The Dark Side of Luxury

Police and Officials Struggle to Stay Ahead of an Avalanche of Cheap Fakes

图片提供：Reuters

MONITA RAJPAL, CNN CORRESPONDENT

This industry of indulgence[1] also has its dark side, or shall I say, its cheap side—goods made to mimic[2] the world's finest products available at bargain basement prices. In some parts of the world, making counterfeit[3] goods is such a big business, it's almost impossible to control. Dan Rivers has more from Bangkok.

DAN RIVERS, CNN CORRESPONDENT

Crushing the counterfeits in Thailand is an industrial process. The country is awash[4] with fake merchandise[5] and the police are making a show of trying to stamp out the problem.

17-F.MP3
17-S.MP3

行业之道　品牌哲学　财经内幕　商海拾趣　环球生活

Notes & Vocabulary

标题扫描

an avalanche of 雪片般的；大量的

avalanche [ˋævəˌlæntʃ] 原意是 "雪崩"，an avalanche of sth. 是指某事物如同雪崩一般，一下子大量出现。

stamp out

杜绝；消除

stamp 在这里作为动词，有阻止不好的事物继续发展的意思，因此词组 stamp out 解释为 "杜绝；消除"。

The country is doing its best to **stamp out** human trafficking.
这个国家尽一切努力要杜绝人口贩卖。

CNN 特派员 莫妮塔·拉吉波

这个放纵欲望的产业也有黑暗的一面，或者该说是廉价的一面——仿冒世界上最精致的产品，再以最低贱的价格出售。在世界某些地区，仿冒品行业的规模非常大，几乎不可能控制。丹·里佛斯从曼谷带来以下报道。

CNN 特派员 丹·里佛斯

在泰国，打击仿冒品是一个工业化的过程。这个国家的伪造商品极为泛滥，以至于警方必须公开展现他们消灭这个问题的决心。

1. **indulgence** [ɪnˋdʌldʒəns]
   n. 沉溺；放纵

2. **mimic** [ˋmɪmɪk]
   v. 模仿；学……的样子
   The insect mimics leaves to hide from predators.

3. **counterfeit** [ˋkaʊntɚˌfɪt]
   adj. 伪造的；假冒的
   Kelly told her friends that her counterfeit Gucci bag was authentic.

4. **awash** [əˋwɔʃ]
   adj. 充斥的；泛滥的
   Since the war began, neighboring countries have been awash in refugees fleeing the fighting.

5. **merchandise** [ˋmɝtʃənˌdaɪz]
   n. 商品；货物

Literally hammering home their message to the Thai media that fake luxury goods will not be tolerated[6] anymore. Well, that's the PR[7] spin[8] here. This rather theatrical[9] performance is from a police general who insists they're doing their best to enforce[10] the law.

But at one of Bangkok's many street markets, we find fake watches are openly on sale. Orders can be placed from a catalogue of counterfeits. One trader told us they sell more than $500 worth of watches in an average week. This stall[11] holder didn't want to show her face. She says she's not doing anything wrong, because she's not selling brand names, even though her merchandise includes watches and bags that look just like well-known western makes.[12]

他们毫不含糊地向泰国媒体表明，往后将不再容忍仿冒品。这是此地的公关宣传手法。这项颇富戏剧性的表演出自一名警察上将，他坚称警方执法已经尽了全力。

但在曼谷为数众多的街道市场里，我们却在其中一处发现摊贩公然贩卖伪表。顾客可以翻阅仿冒品目录订购想要的款式。一名商人向我们透露，他们平均每星期卖出价值超过 500 美元的表。这名摊主不愿露脸。她说她没有做错事，因为她卖的商品没有品牌。但这些手表及提包和西方名牌商品看起来一模一样。

Notes & Vocabulary

hammer home 明确指出；强调

动词 hammer 是"锤击；锤打"，home 当副词是"切中要害地；深入地"。hammer home 表示一再强调某个想法，以求确实传达、深入人心。

- The documentary hammers home the need to protect the environment.
这部纪录片一再强调保护环境的重要性。

其他与 hammer 连用的词组

hammer away

不断要求；接连工作

- The lawyer hammered away at the witness.
那名律师不断地盘问该名证人。

hammer out

经详细讨论后得出结论

- The politicians hammered out a peace treaty.
政治家们经过讨论后得出一条和平条约。

6. **tolerate** [ˈtɑləˌret]
v. 容忍；宽恕
Ben cannot tolerate much pain.

7. **PR** [ˈpiˌɑr]
n. 公共关系（= public relations）

8. **spin** [spɪn]
n. 特殊看法；花招

9. **theatrical** [θiˈætrɪkl]
adj. 夸张的；戏剧性的
Judith's theatrical pleas for attention are beginning to annoy Randal.

10. **enforce** [ɪnˈfɔrs] *v.* 实施；执行
Local police enforced the new curfew.

11. **stall** [stɔl] *n.* 摊位

12. **make** [mek] *n.* 品牌；型；样式

行业之道 | 品牌哲学 | 财经内幕 | 商海拾趣 | 环球生活

This is what happened when police tried to clamp down on copyright infringement[13] in the music industry here a few years ago. You can see why officers might be reluctant[14] to sweep on the lucrative[15] fake watch market, and anyway experts say it's the suppliers, not the retailers, that need to be tackled.[16]

PETER THORN, U.S. EMBASSY

The problem is moving up the chain to actually arresting the manufacturers,[17] closing down the factories where it's being produced.

DAN RIVERS, CNN CORRESPONENT

Many of the fake luxury goods are made outside of Thailand. This is Myanmar, formerly Burma, where

警方在几年前试图打击音乐行业侵害版权的
行为时，发生了画面中的反抗冲突。由此可
以看出，警员为什么没兴趣打击利润丰厚的
伪表市场。而且专家也说，真正该抓的是供
应商，而不是零售商。

美国大使馆 彼得·索恩
问题在于如何追查上游来源，逮捕制造商，
查封生产这些仿冒品的工厂。

CNN 特派员 丹·里佛斯
许多仿冒品的生产地都在泰国境外。这里是
缅甸，仿冒品在这里随处可见。我们在一名

Notes & Vocabulary

move up the chain
向上发展；追溯

chain 是"连锁；连串"，move up the chain 表示沿着某个连续性的事物向上延伸，在文中是指往上游追查仿冒品。

- Bob's suggestion moved up the chain to the company's CEO.
鲍伯的建议往上呈到了公司首席执行官那儿。

其他与 chain 连用的词组

pull/yank one's chain
开玩笑；故意刁难
- Steve pulled his brother's chain by asking when he is finally going to get married.
史蒂夫故意刁难他哥哥，问他何时要结婚。

a ball and chain
牵绊；拖累；〔俚〕妻子
- Fred jokingly introduced his wife as his "ball and chain."
佛烈德开玩笑地说他的太太是他的"枷锁"。

13. **infringement** [ɪnˋfrɪndʒmənt]
n. 违反；侵犯

14. **reluctant** [rɪˋlʌktənt]
adj. 不情愿的；勉强的
David is reluctant to quit his job.

15. **lucrative** [ˋlukrətɪv]
adj. 赚钱的；有利可图的
Mindy received a lucrative offer from a rival company.

16. **tackle** [ˋtækl]
v. 着手对付（或处理）
The president tackled balancing the national budget during his first month in office.

17. **manufacturer** [ˋmænjəˋfæktʃərə]
n. 制造商

行业之道｜品牌哲学｜财经内幕｜商海拾趣｜环球生活

fakes are commonplace.[18] At one distributor[19] we find entire boxes of watches ready for shipment. They're, according to the owner, smuggled[20] through Myanmar into Thailand, where there are plenty of Western tourists.

FRANCOIS GAULIN, U.S. TOURIST
To say that this watch right here does not look nice ... this watch right here looks very beautiful. I mean it's a very nice watch. I mean, you know, you'd have to be crazy to say it's not, but, um, still ...

DAN RIVERS, CNN CORRESPONENT
But it's a fake?

FRANCOIS GAULIN, U.S. TOURIST
But ... Well, I don't know if it's a fake, because I can't prove that, but ...

DAN RIVERS, CNN CORRESPONENT
For 10 bucks it's got to be, right?

FRANCOIS GAULIN, U.S. TOURIST
For 10 bucks I would vouch[21] or say that it's a fake. Yeah, yeah.

DAN RIVERS, CNN CORRESPONENT
So does each fake erode[22] the exclusivity of the real thing?

批发商那里发现了一箱箱准备运走的手表。
业主说这些手表是途经缅甸走私进入泰国
的，因为泰国有许多西方游客。

美国游客　弗朗思瓦·高林

说这块表不好……这块表看起来很漂亮。我
是说，这是一块很好的表，你发神经才会说
这块表不好，可是当然……

CNN 特派员　丹·里佛斯

可是这是仿冒品吧？

美国游客　弗朗思瓦·高林

我不知道是不是仿冒品，因为我也没办法证
明，可是……

CNN 特派员　丹·里佛斯

一块表 10 美元，一定是仿冒的，对吧？

美国游客　弗朗思瓦·高林

只要 10 美元的话，那我敢说一定是仿冒
品。是的，没错。

CNN 特派员　丹·里佛斯

仿冒品会损及真品的独特性吗？

Notes & Vocabulary

18. **commonplace** [ˈkɑmənˌples]
    adj. 司空见惯的；普通的

19. **distributor** [dɪˈstrɪbjutə]
    n. 批发商

20. **smuggle** [ˈsmʌgl]
    v. 走私；非法私运
    Criminals smuggled pirated goods out of the country.

21. **vouch** [vautʃ] *v.* 担保；作证
    The shopkeeper vouched for the item's authenticity.

22. **erode** [ɪˈrod] *v.* 腐蚀；侵蚀
    A series of gaffes and missteps eroded the candidate's support.

行业之道｜品牌哲学｜财经内幕｜商海拾趣｜环球生活

MALA TANGPRASERT, SELECTIVE TRADEMARK UNION, LTD.
If you are walking wearing a genuine[23] Rolex, and see others wearing their fake Rolex, it looks exactly the same. The customer would feel frustrated.

DAN RIVERS, CNN CORRESPONENT
Fighting the fakes must seem like fighting a losing battle. This is just a fraction[24] of the $137 million worth of luxury counterfeit goods that were seized in Thailand in just one year.

So despite all the tough talk and publicity stunts, the reality is that for every fake item destroyed here, there are millions more being churned out in factories. It's going to take more than a steamroller[25] to crush this problem.

商标识别联盟 玛拉·唐普拉塞特

你如果戴着真的劳力士表，结果看到别人戴着仿冒品，而且看起来和真品一模一样。这个消费者一定会觉得很沮丧。

CNN 特派员 丹·里佛斯

打击仿冒品看起来一定像是一场节节败退的战役。泰国一年查获的仿冒奢侈品价值就高达 1.37 亿美元。而查获的只是商品的一小部分。

尽管官方口气强硬，也采用了各种宣传花招，实际上的情形却是，这里每销毁一件仿冒品，工厂又会生产出数百万件。要粉碎这个问题，即使用蒸汽压路机也不够。

Notes & Vocabulary

fight a losing battle
徒劳无功

fight a losing battle 字面意思是"打一场会输的仗"，也就是指所做的事情只是"徒劳无功"而已。

· The government is fighting a losing battle against industrial pollution.
政府与工业污染进行着一场毫无胜算的战争。

与 fight a losing battle 意思相似的词组

make a futile effort
白费力气

· Tim made a futile effort to seal the broken pipe.
提姆折腾了一番还是堵不住那个破掉的水管。

beat the air/wind
白费心思

· Jack is just beating the wind if he thinks he'll win back Julia.
杰克如果以为他能赢回茉莉亚，那根本只是妄想。

churn out 大量制造

churn 原本是指"用搅乳器搅拌"奶油等乳制品，churn out 则是"大量生产"的意思，有不重品质、粗制滥造的含意。

· The factory churns out thousands of fake items every month.
那家工厂每个月会制造出数千个仿冒商品。

23. genuine [ˈdʒɛnjʊɪn]
adj. 真的；非伪造的
Allan bought a genuine Gucci bag for his wife.

24. fraction [ˈfrækʃən]
n. 小部分；些许

25. steamroller [ˈstimˌrolə]
n. 蒸汽压路机

行业之道 | 品牌哲学 | 财经内幕 | 商海拾趣 | 环球生活

Downtown Drilling in Disguise[1]

Going Undercover[2] to Pump up L.A.'s Urban[3] Oil Deposits[4]

图片提供：Reuters

CNN ANCHOR

You may have heard of the ongoing debate in the U.S. on whether to drill offshore for oil. Well, experts say Americans might not need to look that far. Ted Rowlands did some searching in sunny Los Angeles.

TED ROWLANDS, CNN CORRESPONDENT

Driving along Pico Boulevard in Los Angeles, you wouldn't notice. But inside that building with the tower, there's a working oil drill[5] helping to produce more than 900 barrels[6] of oil a day. Take a look at this building from the street. Now look at it from above.

18-F.MP3
18-S.MP3

CNN 主播

您可能听说过，美国国内一直存在着是否该在近海钻油的争论。专家说，美国人可能不必到那么远的地方去寻找石油。记者泰德·罗兰在阳光普照的洛杉矶做了些访查。

CNN 记者 泰德·罗兰

开车驶过洛杉矶市的皮可大道时你不会注意到这件事，但在那栋有座高塔的大楼里却有座正在运作中的钻油机，每天可以生产 900 桶原油。从街道上瞧瞧这栋建筑，再从上空看看它。

Notes & Vocabulary

行业之道 | 品牌哲学 | 财经内幕 | 商海拾趣 | 环球生活

1. **disguise** [dɪsˋgaɪz]
   n.; v. 伪装；假扮；掩饰
   Allan disguised his mailbox as a birdhouse.

2. **undercover** [ˏʌndɚˋkʌvɚ]
   adv. 暗中地；秘密地

3. **urban** [ˋɝbən]
   adj. 都市的；城中的
   Max studied urban planning while in university.

4. **deposit** [dɪˋpɑzət]
   n. 矿床；堆积；沉淀

5. **oil drill** [ɔɪl] [drɪl]
   石油钻井机

6. **barrel** [ˋbærəl]
   n. (汽油、酒等) 大桶；一桶的量

Across Los Angeles, oil production blends into urban life—some of it hidden, some of it out in the open. It's in neighborhoods near baseball fields. Even Beverly Hills High School has oil pumping on campus, disguised as a work of art.

IRAJ ERSHAGHI, UNIVERSITY OF SOUTHERN CALIFORNIA
More than two-thirds of the state is underground.

TED ROWLANDS, CNN CORRESPONDENT
Dr. Iraj Ershaghi is the director of petroleum[7] engineering at USC. He estimates[8] there's more than nine billion barrels of oil still to be had in the Los Angeles Basin—a real opportunity to reduce imports, which he says should not be lost.

IRAJ ERSHAGHI, UNIVERSITY OF SOUTHERN CALIFORNIA
It took millions of years to cook that stuff underground and you can't just walk away from it.

在整个洛杉矶市，石油生产融入了市区生活，有些是隐藏的，有些则是公开显露在外的。棒球场邻近地区有钻油设施，甚至比佛利山高中校园内也有以艺术品外表作为掩饰的钻油设施。

南加州大学 伊拉贾·厄夏吉

加州三分之二以上的地底下都蕴藏着石油。

CNN 记者 泰德·罗兰

伊拉贾·厄夏吉博士是南加州大石油工程学系的系主任。他估计整个洛杉矶盆地仍蕴藏有 90 亿桶的石油。这是减少进口的大好机会，他表示这样的机会不该错失。

南加州大学 伊拉贾·厄夏吉

地底下的石油要数百万年才能生成，你不能就这样置之不理。

Notes & Vocabulary

blend in/into 混合；融入

blend 是"混合；混杂；使交融"的意思，后面用 in 或 into 表示"混合到……中"，有"调和；融入"的意思。blend 本身可当名词指"混合；融合"或"混合物"。

- Because she is shy, Rhonda **blended into** the crowd at the party.
  朗达很害羞，所以混在派对的人群里。

相似词

▶ **mix in** 混合；掺合；来往

▶ **mingle in** 与……交际

out in the open 在户外

open 当名词是指"户外；野外；空地"，out in the open 就是"在户外、在公然可见的地方"，out 可以省略。

- Left **out in the open**, the old car's paint soon became rusty and faded.
  那辆旧车被遗弃在室外，很快就生锈掉漆了。

7. **petroleum** [pə`troliəm]
   n. 汽油；石油

8. **estimate** [`ɛstə,met]
   v. 估计；评量
   Betty estimated the cost of her trip to be around $2,000.

行业之道 ｜ 品牌哲学 ｜ 财经内幕 ｜ 商海拾趣 ｜ 环球生活

TED ROWLANDS, CNN CORRESPONDENT

Maps show a significant part of the Los Angeles Basin is rich in oil, but with so many people living here, getting to it without disrupting lives or the environment requires[9] facilities[10] like the one on Pico. Here, an electric, not diesel drill, does the work. It's capable of going thousands of feet down and up to a mile in any direction.

GREG BROWN, BREITBURN ENERGY PARTNERS

The technology is here to do this sort of a facility in ways that are environmentally very sensitive.[11]

TED ROWLANDS, CNN CORRESPONDENT

While many people are worried about more drilling, it's coming. More than 4,000 applications have been filed[12] already this year for new wells or opening old ones. That's up from a total of 3,000 last year. Oil companies say with more wells, imports go down, tax revenues[13] and jobs go up, and the companies promise not to disturb the neighborhood.

Los Angeles Basin 洛杉矶盆地

位于美国加州南部沿海，长 56 千米、宽 24 千米。属于沉积（sediment-filled）平原（plain），沉积层深度有 11 千米，约在 1.5 万年前的新第三纪（Neogene）形成，因地壳隆起（crustal upheaval）而从海底上升。据推测地层中堆积的微生物（microorganisms）残骸就是在那个时期形成石油的。

洛杉矶市 1892 年发现油源，至今洛杉矶郡内的油井约有 3400 座。以名流和精品知名的比佛利山（Beverly Hills）市内就有 97 座，去年原油产量达 100 万桶。

18-F.MP3 / 18-S.MP3 ▮ *Downtown Drilling in Disguise*

CNN 记者 泰德·罗兰

地图显示洛杉矶盆地中有很大一部分富含石油，但是当地人口如此稠密，既要取得石油，又不对环境造成破坏，就要用到皮可大道上的这种设施。在这里，钻油机是靠电力驱动的，而非柴油。它可以朝地底任何方向钻数千英尺深，最深可达一英里。

布莱德伯恩能源合伙公司 葛雷·格布朗

这项技术能以对环境很友好的方式小心地钻油。

CNN 记者 泰德·罗兰

就在许多人对于钻油量的增加感到忧心之际，钻油计划却大举来袭了。今年已经申报的开掘新油井或重开旧油井项目已达四千多个，较去年一整年的三千个还多。石油公司表示，随着油井数量的增加，进口石油量降低，税收和工作机会将因此增加，石油公司也承诺不会打扰到街坊邻居。

Notes & Vocabulary

rich in sth. 富含

rich 是 "富裕的；丰富的"，后面用介词 in 加上事物表示 "富含……的；……丰富的"。

- **The area is rich in fertile soil and reliable sources of water.**
  那个地区富含肥沃土壤和稳定水源。

9. **require** [rɪˋkwaɪr] *v.* 需要
   Opening a new bank account requires at least one form of identification.

10. **facility** [fəˋsɪlətɪ]
    n. 设施；便利；能力

11. **sensitive** [ˋsɛnsətɪv]
    adj. 敏感的；有知觉的
    These plants do best in the shade because they are sensitive to direct light.

12. **file** [faɪl] *v.* 提出（申请、控告等）
    The secretary filed the company's financial records.

13. **revenue** [ˋrɛvəˌnu]
    n. 收入；税收

行业之道 ｜ 品牌哲学 ｜ 财经内幕 ｜ 商海拾趣 ｜ 环球生活

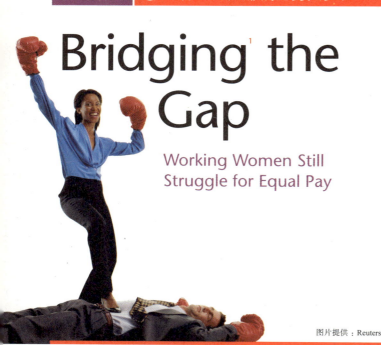

Bridging[1] the Gap

Working Women Still Struggle for Equal Pay

图片提供：Reuters

CNN ANCHOR

Well, same job, different gender,[2] very different pay. That's the result of a new study released in the United States.

CNN ANCHOR

That's more than four decades[3] after the Equal Pay Act was passed. Randi Kaye tried to find out why women and men still aren't paid the same money for the same jobs.

RANDI KAYE, CNN CORRESPONDENT

Wouldn't it be nice if we could all earn a living on the catwalk?[4] Modeling is one of the few careers where women actually earn more than men. In nearly every other field,[5] boys make the bigger bucks.

19-F.MP3
19-S.MP3

CNN 主播

同一份工作，不同性别，薪酬却大不相同。美国的一项新研究刚发布了这个结果。

CNN 主播

这是在《平等薪酬法》通过 40 余年后发生的事。记者蓝迪·凯伊要设法探究为何男性和女性依然同工不同酬。

CNN 特派员 蓝迪·凯伊

如果我们都能在 T 台上讨生活不是很好吗？模特业是少数几个女性酬劳比男性高的行业之一。几乎在所有其他行业中，男性都赚得比女性多。

1. **bridge** [brɪdʒ]
   v. 使……联结；缩短距离
   The translator bridged the language gap.

2. **gender** [ˋdʒɛndɚ] *n.* 性别

3. **decade** [ˋdɛked] *n.* 十年

4. **catwalk** [ˋkæt͵wɔk] *n.* T 台

5. **field** [fild] *n.* 领域

行业之道 ｜ 品牌哲学 ｜ 财经内幕 ｜ **商海拾趣** ｜ 环球生活

CATHERINE HILL, AMERICAN ASSOC. OF UNIVERSITY WOMEN
We found that one year out of college, women were already earning less than their male peers,[6] and that 10 years after college, that gap had widened.[7]

RANDI KAYE, CNN CORRESPONDENT
Researcher Catherine Hill found women earn just 80 percent of what men earn one year out of college. A decade later, their paychecks continue to plummet,[8] down to 69 percent.

CATHERINE HILL, AMERICAN ASSOC. OF UNIVERSITY WOMEN
We're seeing the same kind of gap that we saw for their mothers and grandmothers.

RANDI KAYE, CNN CORRESPONDENT
In the 1960s, Hill says women earned 59 cents on the dollar compared to men. By the '90s, it had jumped to 78 cents. But in the last few years, women's salaries have been stuck right around there. Why does the pay gap still exist?

CATHERINE HILL, AMERICAN ASSOC. OF UNIVERSITY WOMEN
When we have something unexplained[9] that we can't control by any of the things we know affect earnings, it suggests to us discrimination's[10] still a problem.

美国大学妇女协会 凯瑟琳·希尔

我们发现刚踏出大学校园一年之后，女性赚的钱就已经比男性同龄人少了，毕业十年后，两者之间的差距就更大了。

CNN 特派员 蓝迪·凯伊

研究人员凯瑟琳·希尔发现大学毕业一年后，女性的收入就只有男性的八成。十年之后，女性薪酬持续下降，只能达到男性的69%。

美国大学妇女协会·凯瑟琳·希尔

我们目睹的差距和这些人的母亲以及祖母时代的差距是一样的。

CNN 特派员 蓝迪·凯伊

希尔说，20 世纪 60 年代，男性赚一美元，女性只能赚 59 美分，到了 90 年代，女性的薪酬跃升到了 78 美分。但是在过去几年间，女性的薪酬水平就一直停滞不前。为何男女的薪酬差距依旧存在呢？

美国大学妇女协会 凯瑟琳·希尔

当我们看到薪酬会受到某些无法解释的因素的影响，而我们又无法左右这些因素时，就表示歧视的问题依旧存在。

Notes & Vocabulary

earned 59 cents on the dollar

文章中的 earned 59 cents on the dollar 等于 0.59：1，即男性赚一美元，女性赚 59 美分。句子中的 on 是固定用法。

- Compared to their male counterparts, women **earned 70 cents on the dollar**.
  与男性职员相比，女性的薪酬只有男性职员的 70%。

- The company was able to buy out its British rival's stock **at 80 pence on the pound**.
  这家公司以市值股价的 80% 并购了其英国竞争对手。

suggest 显示；表示

suggest 常解释为"提议；建议"，但在这则新闻中的 **suggest** 是"显示；表示"的意思。

- The statistic **suggests** the gender pay gap still exists.
  此数据显示，因性别不同而产生的薪资差异依然存在。

6. **peer** [pɪr] *n.* 同龄人

7. **widen** [ˈwaɪdn̩] *v.* 扩大
   The gap widened between the rich and poor.

8. **plummet** [ˈplʌmət]
   v. 下降；重挫
   The stock's value plummeted.

9. **unexplained** [ˌʌnɪkˈsplend]
   adj. 无法解释的
   The astronomers recorded several unexplained phenomena.

10. **discrimination** [dɪsˌkrɪməˈneʃən]
    n. 歧视

行业之道 品牌哲学 财经内幕 商海拾趣 环球生活

RANDI KAYE, CNN CORRESPONDENT

Is it really discrimination or is it career choices? Women favor[11] education and lower-paying jobs, while men gravitate[12] toward engineering and finance, which pay more. But there is evidence the gap exists even within the same field.

CATHERINE HILL, AMERICAN ASSOC. OF UNIVERSITY WOMEN

Even within people who are doing the same field of study, one year out, we see very large pay differences.

RANDI KAYE, CNN CORRESPONDENT

The gender pay gap varies[13] by state. Here in New York, women earn 82 percent of what men earn. That is just slightly[14] behind West Virginia, which has the smallest pay gap in the country. But in Louisiana, the ladies make just 64 percent of what the guys do. That is the largest gender pay gap in the U.S.

Not only do women get paid less, but there are fewer of them in executive[15] roles. That leaves men with more authority, more involvement[16] in hiring, and yes, setting[17] pay.

Why don't we see more women at the top? Sylvia Ann Hewlett has been tracking[18] gender issues in the workplace[19] for two decades and finds women forced to choose between work and family.

SYLVIA ANN HEWLETT, CENTER FOR WORK-LIFE POLICY

What we are finding is that ambitious,[20] committed[21] women are looking at this—these jobs—and electing really not to go into them. Women are, in a way, deliberately[22] avoiding the very long-hour careers.

CNN 特派员 蓝迪·凯伊

这真的是因为歧视吗？还是因为职业选择的差异？女性喜欢教育和收入较低的工作，而男性则比较倾向于从事工程和财务方面的工作，这类工作的薪酬水平较高。但有证据显示，即使是在同一个领域中，男女之间的薪酬差距也是存在的。

美国大学妇女协会 凯瑟琳·希尔

就连在学校学同一个专业的人，我们都发现他们在毕业一年后的工资差距相当大。

CNN 特派员 蓝迪·凯伊

性别的薪酬差距在各州有所不同。在纽约州，女性的收入是男性的 82%。仅次于全美男女薪酬差距最小的弗吉尼亚州。但在路易斯安那州，女性的收入却只有男性的 64%。这是全美国男女薪酬最悬殊的地区。

女性领的薪水较少，担任主管职务的人数更少。因此男性的权威比较高，并且在人事任用过程中有较高的参与度，进而有权决定薪酬的多寡。

为何我们看不见更多女性担任主管职务呢？研究职场性别议题逾 20 年的西尔维亚·安·休利特发现，女性往往被迫在工作和家庭之间做抉择。

工作生活政策中心 西尔维亚·安·休利特

我们发现有雄心和决心的女性在看待这类主管职务时的态度是，她们选择不去做这样的工作。从某方面来看，女性有意避免从事需要长时间投入的职业。

Notes & Vocabulary

11. **favor** [ˈfevə] v. 偏爱；偏袒
The golfer favors oversized drivers.

12. **gravitate** [ˈɡrævəˌtet] v. 被吸引；倾向
Many young boys gravitate toward sports.

13. **vary** [ˈvɛrɪ] v. 不同；多样变化
Employee salaries varied depending on seniority.

14. **slightly** [ˈslaɪtlɪ] adv. 稍微地

15. **executive** [ɪɡˈzɛkjətɪv] adj. 主管级的
The company is trying to fill several executive positions.

16. **involvement** [ɪnˈvɑlvmənt] n. 涉入；牵扯

17. **set** [sɛt] v. 规定；设定
Management set a salary cap for all employees.

18. **track** [træk] v. 追踪；跟踪
The government tracks unemployment figures.

19. **workplace** [ˈwɜkˌples] n. 工作场所

20. **ambitious** [æmˈbɪʃəs] adj. 有野心的
Ben is part of an ambitious young sales team.

21. **committed** [kəˈmɪtɪd] adj. 坚定的；忠诚的
William is a committed member of the organization.

22. **deliberately** [dɪˈlɪbərətlɪ] adv. 故意地；蓄意地

CATHERINE HILL, AMERICAN ASSOC. OF UNIVERSITY WOMEN
The percentage of female executives, Hewlett says, has dropped from 15 to 14 percent just in the last year.

But 15 to 14 percent doesn't sound like a lot.

SYLVIA ANN HEWLETT, CENTER FOR WORK-LIFE POLICY
Yeah, but it's heading in the wrong direction. It took us about 30 years to get up to that 15 percent. And so, any step back, I think, is very disturbing.[23]

RANDI KAYE, CNN CORRESPONDENT
Can the gap be narrowed? Sure, says Hewlett, by encouraging young women to break into male-dominated[24] fields and by making the work model more female-friendly, allowing women to raise a family and climb the corporate ladder. Only then will the gender pay gap be gone for good.

Equal Pay Act 平等薪资法

act 是"法案；法令"的意思。所谓"平等薪资法"是针对男性与女性薪酬给付不公平（pay inequality）的情况而制定的法令，通常在发达国家（developed countries）较注重这样的问题。

- 最早制定平等薪资法的国家及其时间：
  美国——1963 年
  英国——1970 年
  法国——1972 年

延伸补充

Feminism 女性主义
两性平等的议题与女性主义关系密切，以下补充女性主义的起源及影响：
起源——一般认为从 18 世纪启蒙运动时期（Age of Enlightenment）开始萌芽。
影响——女性投票权（suffrage）、较平等的工资（equitable wages）、提出离婚的主动权（initiate divorce）、安全堕胎（abortion）与结扎（ligation）的权利、获得教育权利等。

19-F.MP3 / 19-S.MP3 ▍ *Bridging the Gap*

CNN 特派员 蓝迪·凯伊

休利特表示，女性主管的比例在去年从 15% 降到了 14%。

但是从 15% 到 14% 听来不算很多吧。

工作生活政策中心 西尔维亚·安·休利特

是，但是正在朝着不良的方向发展。我们花了 30 年的时间才达到 15%。所以，我认为任何倒退都很令人担忧。

CNN 特派员 蓝迪·凯伊

这道鸿沟可以缩小吗？休利特认为当然可以。方法包括鼓励年轻女性进入原本由男性主宰的领域，同时开发出对女性更加方便的工作模式，让女性得以一边照顾家庭，一边在企业中逐步晋升。唯有如此，男女之间的薪酬差距才会有抹平的一天。

Notes & Vocabulary

climb the corporate ladder
获得晋升

corporate 是"公司的；企业的"，ladder 是"梯子"，climb the corporate ladder 照字面来说就是"沿着公司的阶层制度往上爬"，也就是 get promoted，指步步高升的意思。

· Jeff successfully climbed the corporate ladder after graduation.
杰夫在毕业后成功地在公司职位上步步高升。

for good
永远地

for good 又作 for good and all，代表"永远地；永久地"，相当于 permanently、forever。

· Jeremy gave up smoking for good.
杰若米彻底戒烟了。

23. **disturbing** [dɪˋstɜbɪŋ]
    adj. 扰人的；让人烦忧的
    Alex learned several disturbing facts about his new girlfriend.

24. **dominate** [ˋdɑməˌnet]
    v. 支配；统治
    The team dominated its opponent.

Ads That Watch You

The Next Generation of Computerized[1] Billboards[2] Gets Personal

PAULINE CHIOU, CNN ANCHOR

In Japan, when it comes to[3] advertising, the rules of the game are quickly changing. These days, walk past a billboard ad and you're no longer watching it, it is watching you. Pretty frightening. CNN's Kyung Lah reports on a new tailor-made[4] trend that some call intrusive[5] and others, the future of advertising.

KYUNG LAH, CNN INTERNATIONAL CORRESPONDENT

In the world of advertising, you look at the ads, but soon, they'll be watching you. It's a future imagined in the 2002 movie *Minority Report*. Cameras capture and read Tom Cruise's face, then customized[6] ads for his character[7] pop up.

20-F.MP3
20-S.MP3

CNN 主播 邱曼怡

目前日本广告界的游戏规则变得非常快。现在，已经不再是你看广告牌了，而是广告牌看着你。挺吓人的。本台的景兰带来以下报道，介绍一种量身订制的新潮流。对此有些人称之为侵犯隐私，有些人则称之为广告的未来。

CNN 国际特派员 景兰

在广告的世界里，向来都是你看广告。但再过不久，就会变成广告看你了。这样的科幻画面曾经在 2002 年的电影《关键报告》里出现过。摄像机摄取并分析汤姆·克鲁斯的脸，然后播出为他量身定制的广告。

Notes & Vocabulary

rules of the game
游戏规则；共同遵守的准则

字面意思是"游戏规则"，本来是指球赛的规则，引申为某个领域"多数人共同遵守的准则、规矩"，通常和 change 一起使用，表示改变常规。

- Digital photography changed the **rules of the game** for paparazzi.
  数码摄影技术改变了娱乐业记者的游戏规则。

1. **computerized** [kəm`pjutəˌraɪzd]
   adj. 计算机化的；有关计算机的
   Jack displayed his wedding proposal on the computerized billboard in Times Square.

2. **billboard** [`bɪlbɔrd]
   n. 广告牌；告示牌

3. **when it comes to sth.**
   当提到（某事）时
   When it comes to cars, Mike knows his stuff.

4. **tailor-made** [`teləˌmed]
   adj. 特制的；量身定做的
   The film seemed to be tailor-made for my cinematic tastes.

5. **intrusive** [ɪn`trusɪv]
   adj. 侵入的；干扰的
   Many people considered the new security measures to be intrusive.

6. **customized** [`kʌstəmaɪzd]
   adj. 定做的
   The customized car caught everyone's attention.

7. **character** [`kærəktə]
   n. 性格；特征；角色

行业之道 品牌哲学 财经内幕 商海拾趣 环球生活

ELECTRONIC BILLBOARD, MINORITY REPORT
John Anderson, you could use a Guinness right about now!

KYUNG LAH, CNN INTERNATIONAL CORRESPONDENT
That future is now. This billboard sees you, scans your face, then pulls up[8] an ad you'll like.

Here's how this works. When you walk up to the ad, a camera captures your image. The computer figures out if you're a man or a woman and your age. Meanwhile, an age and gender-specific ad rolls. This shows that I'm in my 30s, and I like seasonal pasta.

The computer then determines how interested you are, how long you stay. That data is then recorded for the company. NEC engineer Junko Amagai says the facial recognition[9] technology is accurate[10] to within 10 years of your actual age, and the next-gen[11] system they're testing out is even more age accurate.

"This is a new age of advertising," says Amagai. "We can learn something we never knew from marketing."

The new ads give real-time[12] reactions to street signs, so marketing can be more targeted[13] and more effective. At this retail[14] event in Tokyo, it's capturing worldwide interest. Art Frickus is a consultant[15] visiting from Holland.

Notes & Vocabulary

《关键报告》电子广告牌

约翰·安德森，您现在可以来杯吉尼斯啤酒！

CNN 国际特派员 景兰

这种科幻技术现在已经实现了。这块广告牌能够看见你，扫描你的脸，然后播出你会喜欢的广告。

这种广告牌的原理是这样的。你走到广告牌前面，摄影机会捕捉你的影像，然后通过计算机识别出你的性别和年龄，播出适合你的年龄层与性别的广告。目前显示出我三十几岁，喜欢当季的意大利面。

接着，计算机会根据你在广告前面停留的时间来判断你对这则广告有多感兴趣，再为该广告公司存下这项资料。NEC 的工程师天谷表示，脸部识别技术判断年龄的准确度可达 10 岁以内；而他们目前正在测试的新一代系统，精确度会更高。

"这是广告的新时代，"天谷说："我们可以从营销当中得知我们以前从不会知道的事情。"

新式广告可以为街头广告牌赋予实时反应的能力，因此营销活动能够更准确地锁定目标，也能更有效。东京的这场零售展吸引了全世界的注意力。亚特·弗里克斯是一名来自荷兰的顾问。

8. **pull up** 拉出：调出
   The nurse pulled up the patient's medical record.

9. **recognition** [ˌrɛkəgˋnɪʃən]
   n. 识别；认出；认可；赏识

10. **accurate** [ˋækjurət]
    adj. 正确无误的；准确的
    The Web site is a good source for accurate weather forecasts.

11. **next-gen** [ˋnɛkstˋdʒɛn]
    adj. 下一代的
    The company is working on a next-gen video game console.

12. **real-time** [ˋrilˌtaɪm]
    adj. 实时的；联机立即反应的
    The cable channel provides real-time stock quotes.

13. **targeted** [ˋtɑrgɪtɪd]
    adj. 针对性的；定向的
    Several targeted ads aimed at sports fans were broadcast during the Super Bowl.

14. **retail** [ˋritel] *adj.* 零售的

15. **consultant** [kənˋsʌltənt]
    n. 顾问

行业之道　品牌哲学　财经内幕　商海拾趣　环球生活

ART FRICKUS, HOLLAND CONSULTANT
I believe in one-on-one communication, and all your messages must be relevant. So, that's why I believe in this kind of thing, technology.

KYUNG LAH, CNN INTERNATIONAL CORRESPONDENT
Do you feel a little uneasy though? That it's …

ART FRICKUS, HOLLAND CONSULTANT
No.

KYUNG LAH, CNN INTERNATIONAL CORRESPONDENT
Frickus brushes off[16] privacy concerns or fears that this is Big Brother. NEC, which so far has only tested the digital ads in Japan, says signs warn passersby they're on camera, and images are not saved in the database. In the post 9/11 world, security cameras are everywhere on public streets and malls; facial recognition technology used by governments, even casinos. NEC believes the use of this technology in advertising is just the next step and will soon be common.

Within two to three years, 10 percent of the ads will be like this.

KOSUKE YAMAUCHI, NEC SPOKESMAN
Ten percent of the digital signage.[17]

KYUNG LAH, CNN INTERNATIONAL CORRESPONDENT
Of digital signage will be like this. That's a global prediction. NEC says testing begins in the U.S. this spring: just weeks away to the arrival of the future.

20-F.MP3 / 20-S.MP3 ▌ *Ads That Watch You*

荷兰顾问 亚特·弗里克斯

我注重一对一的沟通，而且所有信息都必须切合需求。所以，我才会认同这种技术。

CNN 国际特派员 景兰

可是，你不会觉得有点不自在吗？毕竟……

荷兰顾问 亚特·弗里克斯

不会。

CNN 国际特派员 景兰

弗里克斯一点都不担心隐私的问题，也不认为这种做法会像老大哥一样随时监视所有人的一举一动。至今为止只在日本测试过这种数码广告的 NEC 指出，广告牌会告知路人他们受到了摄像机的拍摄，而且影像也不会储存在数据库里。在 9·11 事件之后，世界各地的公共街道与购物中心都布满了监视器；不但政府使用脸部识别技术，连赌场也在使用。NEC 认为在广告中运用这种技术只是自然而然的下一步发展，而且很快就会普及。

再过两到三年，10% 的广告都会变成这种广告。

NEC 发言人 山内孝介

10% 的数码广告牌。

CNN 国际特派员 景兰

10% 的数码广告牌都会变成这样。这是他们对全球的预测。NEC 表示，美国的测试将在今年春季展开：距离科幻时代的来临只剩几个星期了。

Notes & Vocabulary

Big Brother
老大哥；大独裁者

出自乔治·韦尔（George Orwell）1949 年出版的名著《1984》。书中描述了一个由单一政党"内党"（Inner Party）统治的"海洋国"（Oceania）。该党的首领被称为 Big Brother "老大哥"，后来引申为过度监控人民的政府。

- The new government security measure led Dan to insist that Big Brother was interfering with his freedom.
  政府新的安全措施让丹坚决地认为老大哥干涉到了他的自由。

16. **brush off** 漠视
Julie usually brushes off any criticism she gets from anyone outside her family.

17. **signage** [ˈsaɪnɪdʒ]
n. 招牌（集合名词）

环球生活

Maiden[1] Flight

Passengers Pay Top Dollar to Soar into History on the A380

图片提供 : Singapore Airlines Public Affairs Department

RICHARD QUEST, CNN BUSINESS TRAVELLER

We're all about to be the first to fly on the commercial flight of the A380. It's been a long time in the making, but now the countdown is over and for business travelers the world around the era of the superjumbo[2] has arrived.

As we settle[3] ourselves in for takeoff, let's put the A380's size into perspective. Compared to a Boeing 747-400, the A380 is five meters taller, nearly four meters longer. It's the same length as seven and a half London buses all in a row.[4] It has an awesome[5] wingspan[6] of 79.8 meters. That's 18 meters wider than the 747, and the plane is certified[7] to carry

Notes & Vocabulary

put sth. into perspective
清楚地了解

perspective 原本是"透视图；透视图法"，**put sth. into perspective** 是把某事物以透视法描绘、呈现出来，比喻"彻底剖析；清楚了解"。**perspective** 还有"观点；看法"及"洞察力"的意思。

· The tragic aftermath of the earthquake put Jennifer's minor hardships into perspective.
地震后的惨状让珍妮弗的困苦生活更显得捉襟见肘。

1. **maiden** [ˈmedn̩] *adj.* 初次的
   The Titanic sunk on its maiden voyage.

2. **superjumbo** [ˈsupɚˌdʒʌmbo] *n.* 超级巨型喷气式客机

3. **settle** [ˈsɛtl̩] *v.* 安顿
   Roger settled into his favorite chair and opened the morning paper.

4. **in a row** 排成一排；一连串
   The football team won four championships in a row.

5. **awesome** [ˈɔsəm] *adj.* 令人敬畏的
   Mandy had an awesome time on her vacation to Aruba.

6. **wingspan** [ˈwɪŋspæn] *n.* 翼展

7. **certify** [ˈsɝtəˌfaɪ] *v.* 证实；担保
   The testing board certified Jill's nursing license.

《商务旅行家》理查德·奎斯特

我们即将成为 A380 商业客机的第一批乘客。这是个等待已久的时刻，但现在倒计时终于结束了。对于世界各地的商务旅客来说，超级巨无霸客机的时代已经来临了。

在我们坐下来准备起飞的同时，且让我们好好了解一下 A380 的大小。和波音 747-400 型客机比较起来，A380 的高度多了 5 米，长度多了将近 4 米。A380 的长度等于 7.5 辆伦敦巴士排成一列。其翼展也达到惊人的 79.8 米，比波音 747 宽了 18 米。而且，A380 经过认证，可以搭载 800 名以上的乘

more than 800 people, although most airlines will only have around 500 passengers. So, there's lots of space for airlines to play with, and Singapore Airlines is the first to show how this extra room can be put to use. The A380 is no longer a blank canvas.

When all is said and done, this is a plane that's designed to get us from one side of the world to the other. Its range[8] means it can connect dots more than 15,000 kilometers apart. So, what's on board that helps passengers while away the time? There was plenty to eat and drink and watch, but no bars, casinos[9] or gyms promised by other airlines. Instead, the space has been given to passengers.

As we move 'round the plane, this is a good chance to hear from the men and women who actually work on board.[10]

How long have you been flying?

客，只不过大多数航空公司只会搭载 500 人左右。因此，飞机上将有许多空间可供航空公司自行运用。新加坡航空是第一家展现这些额外空间运用成果的航空公司。A380 不再是一张空白的画布。

话说回来，A380 毕竟还是一架运载我们从世界一端飞往另一端的飞机。其续航力长达 1.5 万千米。那么，飞机上有哪些设施能够帮助旅客打发时间呢？食物饮料都不缺，也有许多节目可看，但没有其他航空公司承诺提供的酒吧、赌场或者健身房。新加坡航空把多余的空间都回馈给了旅客。

我们在飞机上走动参观，这可是采访实际在飞机上工作的人员的好机会。

你在飞机上工作有多久了？

Notes & Vocabulary

put to use 利用；运用
put 有"使从事；用于；使受到"的意思，例如 put to the test "使受试验"、put to death "处死"，而 put to use 则表示"使用；利用"。

- James put to use his first aid training when he came upon the traffic accident.
  詹姆士发生车祸时用上了他的急救训练知识。

blank canvas 空白一片
指未上颜料的"空白油画布"，常用来比喻充满各种可能性的事物，例如未来的人生、未定案的计划等。

when all is said and done
做尽一切；终究
字面上的意思是"当所有该说和该做的都完成之时"，常用在说完前言，准备说出重点的时候，或表示考虑过一切后得出的结论。

- When all was said and done, Wendy realized that she could not save her marriage.
  当温迪做了所有的尝试之后，她明白已经无法挽回她的婚姻了。

while away 消磨（时间）
while 在这里当动词，常与 away 连用，是指闲散、轻松地度过时间，即"消磨、打发时间"的意思。

- Norm whiled away the afternoon reading in his hammock.
  诺玛整个下午都在吊床上看书消磨时光。

8. range [rendʒ]
   n. 最大航程；续航力

9. casino [kə`sino] n. 赌场

10. on board [ɑn] [bɔrd]
    在飞机（或船、火车）上

行业之道　品牌哲学　财经内幕　商海拾趣　环球生活

UNIDENTIFIED SINGAPORE AIRLINES HOSTESS
About 11 years plus,[11] coming to 12.

RICHARD QUEST, CNN BUSINESS TRAVELLER
Will you remember today?

UNIDENTIFIED SINGAPORE AIRLINES HOSTESS
Of course! Probably for the rest of my life.

RICHARD QUEST, CNN BUSINESS TRAVELLER
As I move up towards the nose, it becomes clear it takes a lot of people to make this plane fly, one person particularly.

How many times have you actually flown this plane with a full load of passengers at the back?

A380 FIRST COMMERCIAL FLIGHT PILOT, SINGAPORE AIRLINES
This is the first day. This is the first day on the 380 where I have so many passenger[s] onboard this flight. Before today, it was either [an] empty aircraft, we train on the aircraft, there was even no seat[s] in the cabin, just bare wires.

RICHARD QUEST, CNN BUSINESS TRAVELLER
At the very front, just behind where the captain sits, are the luxury first-class suites[12] with the now-famous double beds. There's really only one question that most passengers are asking on the plane: "How much did you pay for your seat?" Because, in a unique way of selling 'em off, Singapore Airlines did it by auction.[13] In economy, some had got a bargain.[14]

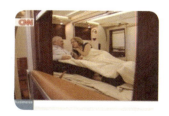

不知名的新加坡航空女空乘人员

差不多 11 年多，快 12 年了。

《商务旅行家》理查德·奎斯特

你会记住今天这个日子吗？

新加坡航空女空乘人员

当然会！大概一辈子都不会忘记。

《商务旅行家》理查德·奎斯特

往机头方向走，就会发现这架飞机需要许多
人员分工合作才能升空。其中一个人更是特
别重要。

你有几次驾驶这架飞机时后面真的是满载乘
客呢？

新加坡航空 A380 商业首航机长

这是第一次。这是我第一次驾驶 A380 搭载
这么多乘客。以前我们在这架飞机上受训的
时候，机舱内部完全是空的，连座位都没
有，只有空荡荡的电线。

《商务旅行家》理查德·奎斯特

在最前端，就在机长的座位后面，是豪华的
头等舱，里面设置有现在已经相当著名的双
人床。飞机上大多数乘客都互相询问同一
个问题："你买的机票多少钱？"因为新加
坡航空很特别地用拍卖的方式销售这个班机
的机票。有不少人在经济舱的机票上捡了便
宜。

11. **plus** [plʌs] *adj.* 多一点的；外加的
Brad expects to spend eight years plus
studying to become a doctor.

12. **suite** [swit] *n.* 客舱；套房

13. **auction** [ˈɔkʃən] *n.* 拍卖

14. **bargain** [ˈbɑrgən]

n. 便宜购买；优惠

行业之道　品牌哲学　财经内幕　商海拾趣　**环球生活**

UNIDENTIFIED ECONOMY-CLASS PASSENGER
The guy in front of me paid $2,700 and I paid $2,650, so I thought I won. I was happier than hell.

RICHARD QUEST, CNN BUSINESS TRAVELLER
In business class, though, others had to pay much, much more.

UNIDENTIFIED MALE BUSINESS-CLASS PASSENGER
We paid 15,000 U.S. for the two seats.

RICHARD QUEST, CNN BUSINESS TRAVELLER
The question then becomes, was it worth it?

UNIDENTIFIED FEMALE BUSINESS-CLASS PASSENGER
Are you kidding?

UNIDENTIFIED MALE BUSINESS-CLASS PASSENGER
Of course.

UNIDENTIFIED FEMALE BUSINESS-CLASS PASSENGER
It's an atmosphere[15] that I don't think you'll ever feel again on an aircraft.

UNIDENTIFIED MALE BUSINESS-CLASS PASSENGER
Yeah.

RICHARD QUEST, CNN BUSINESS TRAVELLER
And at the front end for the brand-new first-class suites, prices were sky high.

经济舱乘客

我前面那个人花了 2700 美元，我花了 2650 美元，所以我想我赢了。真是乐翻了。

《商务旅行家》理查德·奎斯特

但在商务舱，有些人则是付了远超过一般票价的价钱。

商务舱男性乘客

我们买这两个座位的机票花了 1.5 万美元。

《商务旅行家》理查德·奎斯特

接下来的问题就是，值得吗？

商务舱女性乘客

你开玩笑吗？

商务舱男性乘客

当然值得。

商务舱女性乘客

我认为以后再也不可能在飞机上感受到这种气氛了。

商务舱男性乘客

没错。

《商务旅行家》理查德·奎斯特

前端全新头等舱的机票更是天价。

Notes & Vocabulary

15. atmosphere [ˈætməˌsfɪr] *n.* 气氛

行业之道｜品牌哲学｜财经内幕｜商海拾趣｜环球生活

UNIDENTIFIED MALE FIRST-CLASS PASSENGER
$10,100.

RICHARD QUEST, CNN BUSINESS TRAVELLER
The star bidder was Julian Haywood, a 38-year-old
Internet millionaire who paid $100,000 for what is
always the most coveted[16] seat on the plane.

JULIAN HAYWOOD, TOP BIDDER
Well, it's a chance to be in a small piece of aviation[17]
history, it's a chance to give to three excellent
charities,[18] and it's a chance to experience this. It's …
the atmosphere today is turbocharged. It's fun.

Airbus A380 空中的巨无霸

机 体
机身长 73 米，翼展 83 米，宽度 5.6 米，高度 24.2
米，为双层座舱（double-decker）飞机，新加坡航空
A380 载客量（capacity）为 471 人。

过 程
第一架原型机（prototype）于 2005 年 1 月 18 日在
法国图卢兹（Toulouse）机场首度亮相，4 月 27 日首
次飞行，11 月中旬展开全球宣传及长途（long-haul）
测试飞行。之后因线路（wiring）问题延期三次交机，
直至 2007 年 10 月终于交机给新加坡航空，并于 10
月 25 日进行商业首航。

头等舱男性乘客

　　1.01 万美元。

《商务旅行家》理查德·奎斯特

　　出价最高的是朱利安·海伍德，这位 38 岁的网络巨富花了 10 万美元买下飞机上最受垂涎的座位。

最高价得标者 朱利安·海伍德

　　利用这个机会，不但能够参与到航空业的这个历史性时刻中、捐款给 3 个杰出的慈善团体，也可以体验这次飞行，还有今天热烈的气氛。真的是欢乐无穷。

turbocharge
增强；加强
名词 turbocharger 原来是指"涡轮增压器"，动词 turbocharge 则是"装配涡轮增压器"，在口语中则比喻"大幅提高"表现或品质。文中是说在首航班机上的气氛非常兴奋高昂。

· Bruce **turbocharged** his computer with a new CPU and graphics card.
布鲁斯用新的 CPU 和显卡提升了他计算机的性能。

16. **coveted** [ˈkʌvɪtɪd]
    adj. 渴望得到的
    Helga won the coveted first place trophy in the pie baking contest.

17. **aviation** [ˌeviˈeʃən] *n.* 航空

18. **charity** [ˈtʃɛrəti] *n.* 慈善团体

行业之道 ｜ 品牌哲学 ｜ 财经内幕 ｜ 商海拾趣 ｜ 环球生活

Toshiba Introduced Fuel-Cell Phone

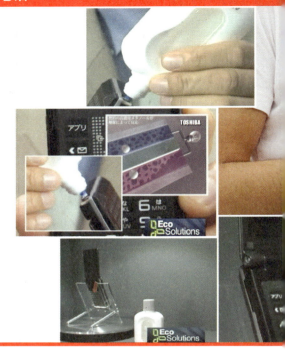

The Japanese company Toshiba recently unveiled[1] a prototype[2] of its new fuel-cell cell phone. Toshiba says customers can have more talk time by powering up their cell phones with methanol.[3] Just by adding a few pumps of the liquid, the phones can be juiced up[4] with electricity through a chemical reaction involving the methanol, water and air. Dr. Fumio Ueno, a Toshiba Technology executive, says these new phones can offer up to six hours of talk time, nearly double that provided by many conventional[5] lithium[6] batteries. Toshiba says the phone could be commercially available in a year or two.

22-F.MP3
22-S.MP3

日本东芝公司日前推出一款使用新式燃料电池的手机。东芝表示，顾客使用甲醇来帮手机的电池充电后，便能享用更长的通话时间。只要挤入几滴甲醇，手机便能通过甲醇、水和空气引发的化学反应充饱电力。在东芝科技担任高层主管的上野文绪博士表示，这些新电话可以提供最长 6 小时的通话时间，比传统锂电池所能提供的通话时间多出将近一倍。东芝表示，该款电话可以在一或两年内上市销售。

Notes & Vocabulary

1. **unveil** [ˌʌnˋvel]
v. 发表；公开；揭露
The car manufacturer unveiled its new hybrid model.

2. **prototype** [ˋprotəˌtaɪp]
n. 原型；模型

3. **methanol** [ˋmɛθəˌnɔl] n. 甲醇

4. **juice up** [dʒus] [ʌp]
使有精神；使活跃
The driver juiced up the batteries of his electric car.

5. **conventional** [kənˋvɛnʃənl]
adj. 常见的；普遍的
Will avoids conventional approaches to problem solving.

6. **lithium** [ˋlɪθɪəm] n. 锂

201

Baseball's Cheating Champs [1]

Playing Fast and Loose with the Rules Started Long Before the Steroid[2] Scandal[3]

图片提供：Reuters

CNN ANCHOR

Well, there's no doubt that the steroid scandal has stained[4] the sport's reputation,[5] but when you look at the big picture, maybe people shouldn't be so surprised. There was cheating in baseball long before there were drugs on the diamond.[6] Jonathon Mann has some Insight.

23-F.MP3
23-S.MP3

Notes & Vocabulary

标题扫描

play fast and loose with
玩弄；胡搞

fast and loose 是指 "反复无常；轻率"，经常与动词 play 搭配，后面可用介词 with 加事物，表示 "玩弄；耍弄"，若加上人则有 "欺骗某人感情" 的意思。

· Lois always plays fast and loose with the rules.
  罗伊斯老是玩弄规则。

the big picture 整体；大范围

big picture 与 detail "细节" 相反，是指某事物所属的 "整体范围"，类似中文说的 "宏观"。look at the big picture 是表示从某事物的整体发展、影响、背景等来观察。

· When one looks at the big picture, the economy doesn't seem so bad.
  就大环境来看，经济状况似乎没那么糟。

CNN 主播

类固醇丑闻毫无疑问已经玷污了棒球运动的名声（注），但是当你从大环境来看这件事时，或许就不应该觉得惊讶了。早在禁药在棒球场内出现之前，棒球运动就已经有舞弊的现象出现了。强纳森·曼恩要为我们带来内幕报道。

1. champ [tʃæmp]
   n.【口】冠军；优胜者

2. steroid [ˈstɪrˌɔɪd] n. 类固醇

3. scandal [ˈskændl̩] n. 丑闻；丑事

4. stain [sten] v. 玷污；败坏
   The scandal stained the actor's clean-cut reputation.

5. reputation [ˌrɛpjəˈteʃən]
   n. 名声；名誉

6. diamond [ˈdaɪəmənd]
   n. 棒球场；内野

注：美国前参议员米切尔经过 12 个月的调查后提出一份报告，点名 86 位退役和现役美国职棒大联盟球员曾使用禁药。该报告称为 "米切尔报告"（Mitchell Report）。名单中包括新出炉的全垒打王邦兹、名投克莱门斯与派提特及多位 MVP 及明星赛选手。大联盟主席塞利格表示会严肃处分，美国国会也决定介入调查。

JONATHAN MANN, INSIGHT

Americans love baseball, and as they say, love is blind, which is why in the current controversy[7] it's easy to overlook[8] the long and colorful history of cheating in the game. So, here's a little baseball cheating 101.

Let's start with the ball itself and the classic, everybody knows it, first-day-of-school kind of cheating. If you change the surface of the baseball, it actually flies differently, even erratically.[9] All-time[10] champ at this, probably Hall of Famer Gaylord Perry. He used to rub on a little Vaseline that he kept under the brim[11] of his cap. Extra points if you refrigerate[12] the ball in a moist[13] environment. Then you get a kind of humid, heavy ball that won't fly as far.

The bat—another classic. Drill out the center of a bat and replace it with cork,[14] you get a lighter, faster swing.[15] All-time champ? Well, let's give that to Norm Cash who won the batting title back in 1961 using a corked bat the entire season. Advanced placement, if you add extra layers of lacquer[16] to the surface of a bat, you can make the wood almost as hard as metal, and really hit that ball.

Then let's look at the field. Groundskeepers[17] can help the home team with the way they paint the lines on the field, for example. So what would be fair balls go foul[18] or the batter's box is just a little bit bigger. All-time champs at that were actually people you've probably never heard of called the Bossard

《内幕报道》强纳森·曼恩

美国人喜爱棒球，而有人说爱是盲目的，这就是为何在当前的争议下，人们很容易就会忽视棒球运动既漫长又包罗万象的舞弊史。所以在此要为大家介绍一些棒球舞弊的常见把戏。

咱们就从球本身谈起吧。这也是人尽皆知的经典舞弊方式，那种在入学第一天就会使用的作弊手法。如果你改变棒球的表面，球的飞行轨迹就会改变，甚至会乱跑。最擅长此道的恐怕是名人堂球员盖洛·派瑞。从前他会在球上抹上一点凡士林，凡士林是事先涂在帽檐下的。如果想达到更棒的效果，就先将球在一个湿气重的环境中冻一会儿，由此一来球会变得潮湿、沉重，而且飞不远。

球棒，另一种经典舞弊方式。把球棒的中心挖空，用软木塞来填充，由此一来球棒会变轻，挥棒速度会变快。个中高手？咱们把这座奖杯颁给 1961 年的打击王诺曼·凯什。当年他一整个球季使用的都是软木塞棒。更进一步的舞弊方式，如果你在球棒表面多上一层漆，球棒的硬度就几乎可以媲美金属，可以将球击得老远。

再来瞧瞧球场。举例来说，场务人员可以通过帮场地画线的方式助主场球队一臂之力。原本的界内会因此变成界外，或者打击区会变得稍大一些。最擅长此道的其实是你恐怕未曾听说过的，叫"波萨德家族"的一群

Notes & Vocabulary

Hall of Famer
名人堂的成员

Hall of Fame 即"名人堂"，是指收藏名人奖杯或纪念品的展览馆，后来则变成贡献卓著的各界代表人物，例如运动员。Fame 词尾改成 –er 就是指"名列名人堂的人"。

7. **controversy** [ˈkɑntrəˌvɚsɪ]
   n. 争议；争论

8. **overlook** [ˌovɚˈlʊk]
   v. 忽视；忽略
   Norah overlooks her boyfriend's many flaws.

9. **erratically** [ɪˈrætɪk]ɪ]
   adv. 不定地；怪异地

10. **all-time** [ˈɔlˌtaɪm]
    adj. 空前的；创纪录的
    Vincent is the all-time worst liar that Danielle has ever known.

11. **brim** [brɪm]
    n. 帽边；（杯、碗）边缘

12. **refrigerate** [rɪˈfrɪdʒɚˌret]
    v. 冷却；冷藏；冷冻
    Andy refrigerated the leftover turkey.

13. **moist** [mɔɪst] *adj.* 湿润的；潮湿的
    Alice slipped on a moist spot on the floor.

14. **cork** [kɔrk] *n.* 软木

15. **swing** [swɪŋ] *n.* 挥棒；挥动

16. **lacquer** [ˈlækɚ] *n.* 亮漆

17. **groundskeeper** [ˈgraʊndzˌkipɚ]
    n. 场务员

18. **foul** [faʊl] *adj.* 犯规的；恶臭的
    The batter hit a foul ball.

family. Over three generations in Cleveland and then in Chicago, too, they performed[19] tricks like watering down the field and softening the baseline paths so players couldn't get to top speed. They also actually moved the outfield[20] fences in and out to favor[21] their own guys.

Then finally there are the drugs. Not the hard stuff like steroids, but stranger stuff. There was a Yankees pitcher back in the '50s or '60s, I guess it was, who used to try to intimidate[22] hitters by playing drunk. The all-time champ here though, Dock Ellis, who threw a no-hitter[23] back in 1970 on LSD. He says the scariest moment in his career was the one time he tried to pitch sober.[24] Serious stuff, but you know, it really is just a game.

名人棒球语录

"It ain't over till it's over."
"球赛结束时才算真的结束。"—— 前扬基队投手约吉·贝拉（Yogi Berra）

"Whoever wants to know the heart and mind of America had better learn baseball."
"想了解美国心理与精神的人，最好学学棒球。"——历史学家杰可·巴森（Jacques Barzun）

"You owe it to yourself to be the best you can possibly be—in baseball and in life."
"不尽可能做到最好就是对不起你自己——不论是棒球还是人生。"

"Baseball is almost the only place in life where a sacrifice is really appreciated."
"棒球场大概是人生中唯一一个做了牺牲真的会被人感激的地方。"

"You gotta be a man to play baseball for a living, but you gotta have a lot of little boy in you, too."
"你必须是个男人才能靠打棒球讨生活，但你也必须让自己的内心保留有童真。"
——前道奇队补手罗伊·坎帕内拉（Roy Campanella）

"Life is like a baseball game. When you think a fastball is coming, you gotta be ready to hit the

人。在长达三代人的时间里，这家人先是在克里夫兰，后来在芝加哥玩弄一些把戏，例如将场地和垒线浇湿、浇软，让球员无法全速驰骋。他们也会将外野的篱笆移近移远，以便偏袒自己喜欢的球员。

最后是禁药。这里指的不是类固醇这类强效禁药，而是些怪东西。20 世纪五六十年代好像有一位扬基队的投手，他会靠酒醉上场投球来恫吓击球手。但是靠禁药舞弊的第一等高手是达克·艾利斯，他在 1970 年靠 LSD 迷幻药投出一场无安打比赛。他说他球员生涯中最恐怖的时刻，是有一回他尝试在清醒的情况下投球。这听来很严重，但你要知道，棒球毕竟只是一种游戏。

curve."
"人生就像一场棒球赛，当你认为来得是个快速直球时，就要做好打曲线球的准备。"——球迷 Jaja Q.

Notes & Vocabulary

water down
稀释；用水浸润；减弱
water 在这里当动词，指"倒水，灌水"，water down 在文中表示让水渗透到土里。另外，该短语还可以引申出抽象的意思，表示"让……减弱、趋缓"，例如程度、强度、效果等。
· Lillian watered down her criticism of the sales staff.
莉莉安把她对业务人员的批评修饰得婉转了一点。

19. **perform** [pɚˋfɔrm]
v. 执行；做；表现
The stock performed well in the third quarter.

20. **outfield** [ˋautˏfild] n. 外野；外场

21. **favor** [ˋfevɚ] v. 偏袒
Many financial planners favor investing in index funds rather than individual stocks.

22. **intimidate** [ɪnˋtɪmədet]
v. 威吓；胁迫
The bully intimidated the other students into giving him their lunch money.

23. **no-hitter** [ˏnoˋhɪtɚ]
n. 无安打比赛

24. **sober** [ˋsobɚ]
adj. 神志清醒的；未沾酒或毒品的
Rob has been sober for nearly 10 years.

行业之道　品牌哲学　财经内幕　商海拾趣　环球生活

Terror at 37,000 Feet

Near Disaster Illustrates[1] the Dangers of Volcanic Ash

图片提供：Reuters

ANDERSON COOPER, AC 360°

Now a look at the danger the volcanic ash poses for airplanes. Boeing tells us in the past 30 years, more than 90 jet-powered commercial[2] airplanes have encountered[3] clouds of volcanic ash and suffered damage as a result.

Tonight we have the frightening story of one flight. Up Close, Randi Kaye with the nightmare at 37,000 feet.

RANDI KAYE, CNN CORRESPONDENT

This documentary[4] from National Geographic recreates the terrifying-but-true ordeal[5] of a British Airways jet caught in a cloud of volcanic ash.

Notes & Vocabulary

《360° 全面视野》安德森·库柏

现在来看看火山灰对航班造成的威胁。波音公司告诉我们，过去 30 年来有超过 90 架次的商业航班曾遭遇过火山灰云，且飞机因此受到了损伤。

今晚我们要来讲关于一架航班的吓人故事。《深入聚焦》的兰迪·凯依要为我们报道这一场在 37 000 英尺高空上演的"恶夜惊魂记"。

CNN 特派员 兰迪·凯依

这部由国家地理频道制作的纪录片重现了一段恐怖但真实的磨难：一架英航喷气式飞机被火山灰云困住的画面。

1. **illustrate** [ˈɪləsˌtret]
   v. 说明；阐释；图解
   The bad bites that Kevin received illustrate the need for carrying insect spray when you hike.

2. **commercial** [kəˈmɝʃəl]
   adj. 商用的；商业的；商务的
   The scientist who created the new substance hopes that it will have commercial applications.

3. **encounter** [ɪnˈkauntɚ]
   v. 遭遇；碰到
   If you encounter a snake on the path, do not go near it.

4. **documentary** [ˌdɑkjəˈmɛntərɪ]
   n. 纪录片

5. **ordeal** [ɔrˈdiəl]
   n. 苦难；严峻考验；折磨

June 24th, 1982, Flight 009 from London to Australia. The radar says expect a smooth[6] flight, but suddenly inside there's reason to panic.[7]

BETTY TOOTELL FERGUSON, PASSENGER, BA FLIGHT 009
I noticed that thick smoke was pouring[8] into the cabin through the vents[9] above the windows.

GRAHAM SKINNER, CHIEF STEWARD, BA FLIGHT 009
The acrid[10] smoke was at the back of your throat, up your nose, in your eyes.

RANDI KAYE, CNN CORRESPONDENT
They are 37,000 feet above the Indian Ocean when the engines ignite.[11]

UNIDENTIFIED BOY, BA FLIGHT 009
Dad, the engine's on fire.

BETTY TOOTELL FERGUSON, PASSENGER, BA FLIGHT 009
There were huge flames coming out of the back of the engines, 20, some people said 40, feet long.

RANDI KAYE, CNN CORRESPONDENT
In about a minute and a half, all four of the Boeing 747's engines fail.[12]

CAPT. ERIC MOODY, PILOT, BA FLIGHT 009
Engine failure. Number four. Fire action, number four.

None of us believed it was happening.

1982 年 6 月 24 日，009 号班机从伦敦飞往澳大利亚。雷达显示这将会是一趟平稳的航程，但机舱内却突然出现了令人恐慌的理由。

英航 009 班机乘客 贝蒂·图特·佛格森

我注意到有浓烟从窗户上方的通风口灌进机舱里。

英航 009 班机座舱长 葛拉罕·史金纳

呛鼻的烟雾进到了我们的喉咙、鼻腔和眼睛里。

CNN 特派员 兰迪·凯依

引擎着火时，班机正在印度洋上空 37 000 英尺处。

英航 009 班机 不知名男孩

爸，引擎起火了。

英航 009 班机乘客 贝蒂·图特·佛格森

熊熊的火焰从引擎后方窜出，足足有 20 英尺高，甚至有人说有 40 英尺。

CNN 特派员 兰迪·凯依

大约一分半钟后，该架波音 747 客机的四个引擎全都熄火了。

英航 009 班机机长 艾瑞克·穆迪

四号引擎故障。四号引擎着火。

我们没人相信会发生这种事。

6. smooth [smuð]
   adj. 平顺的；平稳的；顺利的
   This cream helps keep the skin on my hands soft and smooth.

7. panic [ˈpænɪk]
   v. 恐慌；惊慌；惊恐
   The boy panicked when he fell in the river because he did not know how to swim.

8. pour [por]
   v. 大量漫入、涌入；倾泻
   Steam poured out the door of the locker room as many of the team members were showering.

9. vent [vɛnt] *n.* 通风口；排气孔

10. acrid [ˈækrəd]
    adj. 刺鼻的；刺激的
    The water has a slightly acrid taste, but it is safe to drink.

11. ignite [ɪgˈnaɪt]
    v. 点燃；开始燃烧
    You will have to use a match to ignite the gas stove, as the electric starter is not working.

12. fail [fel] *v.* 故障；失灵
    The basement of the house became flooded after the pump failed.

RANDI KAYE, CNN CORRESPONDENT

What Captain Moody doesn't realize is that he's actually flying through volcanic ash from Mount Galunggung in Indonesia. The ash, made up of[13] tiny bits of glass, is drawn into the engine. It melts and gloms[14] onto the engine parts instead of passing through, choking[15] the engine to death. The Boeing 747 is dropping from the night sky heading straight for the Indian Ocean. They are about six miles up, about a half hour from crashing into the sea.

CAPT. ERIC MOODY, PILOT, BA FLIGHT 009

Mayday, mayday, mayday, speed bird nine, we've lost all four engines.

RANDI KAYE, CNN CORRESPONDENT

Captain Moody warns the nearly 250 passengers to prepare for an emergency landing.

CAPT. ERIC MOODY, PILOT, BA FLIGHT 009

And I said, "Good evening again, ladies and gentlemen. This is your captain speaking. All four en … we have a small problem in that all four engines have failed. We're doing our utmost[16] to keep… to get them going. I trust you're not in too much distress."[17]

RANDI KAYE, CNN CORRESPONDENT

Passengers begin to accept they may not survive.[18]

UNIDENTIFIED MALE, BA FLIGHT 009

Ma, in trouble. Plane going down.

CNN 特派员 兰迪·凯依

穆迪机长不知道他其实正在穿越印度尼西亚嘉能根火山喷发出来的火山灰。这些由细小玻璃组成的灰被吸入了引擎中，它们没有穿过引擎，而是融化并附着在引擎零件上，造成引擎失去动力。这架波音 747 客机从夜空中坠落，直冲向印度洋。当时飞机的高度大约 6 英里，约半个小时就会坠落海底了。

英航 009 班机机长 艾瑞克·穆迪

求救、求救、求救，009 号班机的四个引擎全部失去动力。

CNN 特派员 兰迪·凯依

穆迪机长警告近 250 名乘客为紧急迫降做好准备。

英航 009 班机机长 艾瑞克·穆迪

于是我说："各位先生女士、再一次跟您道晚上好，我是机长。四个引擎全都……我们遇到一个小问题，四个引擎全都失去动力了，我们正在尽全力……启动引擎，我相信各位不会有太大的危险。"

CNN 特派员 兰迪·凯依

乘客们开始接受他们可能会丧命的事实。

英航 009 班机 不知名男子

妈，遇到麻烦了，飞机正在坠落。

Notes & Vocabulary

mayday
无线电通讯的命危求救代号
从法文 m'aider "请前来救援" 演变而来，是国际性的无线电通讯求救代号，表示碰到命危的紧急状况，请立刻前来支援。发信号时一定要连续讲三次，以免受到干扰听不清楚。空军、消防队、运输机构等都会使用。

13. **(be) made up of**
由……组合、构成
A very simple glue made up of flour and water was used to create the paper artwork.

14. **glom** [glɑm]
v. 黏住；瞬间紧紧吸附
Thick weeds in the lake glommed onto the propeller of the boat and caused it to stop.

15. **choke** [tʃok] *v.* 窒息；阻塞
You need to eat slower, because otherwise you could choke.

16. **do one's utmost**
尽全力；尽所能
Although the firefighters did their utmost to save the building, it was destroyed in the fire.

17. **distress** [dɪˋstrɛs]
n. 危难；不幸

18. **survive** [səˋvaɪv]
v. 从……逃生；幸存；存活
The aid group tried to relocate those victims who survived the earthquake.

行业之道 品牌哲学 财经内幕 商海拾趣 环球生活

CHARLES CAPEWELL, PASSENGER, BA FLIGHT 009
We'll do best for the boys. We love you. Sorry, Pa.

RANDI KAYE, CNN CORRESPONDENT
The jet sails through the sky like a glider.[19] Still
unaware of[20] the ash, the crew glides low enough to
escape it.

Captain Moody considers landing in the ocean. But
then at 13,000 feet, the crew gets all four engines
started again. They'd had a chance to cool, and the
ash had broken away.[21] One quickly fails again. Still,
he lands British Airways Flight 009 safely in Jakarta,
Indonesia.

Almost 27 years later after his heroic[22] flight, Capt.
Eric Moody, now retired, tells us it's smart to keep
airplanes away from volcanic ash. He wouldn't want
to fly through it again.

24-F.MP3 / 24-S.MP3 ▎ *Terror at 37,000 Feet*

英航 009 班机乘客 查尔斯·凯普威尔

我们会尽全力救孩子们的。我们爱你，抱歉了，爸。

CNN 特派员 兰迪·凯依

这架飞机像滑翔机一般滑过天际。机组人员仍浑然不知有火山灰这件事，他们将飞机滑翔至极低的空域后刚好逃出了火山灰云。

穆迪机长考虑要在海上降落，但高度到了13 000 英尺时，机组人员再次发动起了四个引擎。他们有了喘息的机会，且火山灰已经散去。其中一个引擎很快又再次熄火，但他仍安全地将英航 009 号班机降落在印度尼西亚雅加达。

已经退休的穆迪机长，在结束该趟英勇的飞行任务近 27 年后告诉我们，让飞机远离火山灰是聪明的做法。他可不想再次驾机飞越火山灰了。

19. **glider** [ˈɡlaɪdə]
   n. 滑翔机；滑翔翼

20. **unaware of**
   没注意；没察觉；不知情
   The people in the movie theater were unaware of the bad storm approaching.

21. **break away**
   脱离；挣脱；摆脱
   Water caused parts of the old brick wall to break away over time.

22. **heroic** [hɪˈroɪk]
   adj. 英雄的；英勇的
   The soldier's heroic deeds in the battle won him a medal.

行业之道 ｜ 品牌哲学 ｜ 财经内幕 ｜ 商海拾趣 ｜ 环球生活

The Cupboard[1] Is Bare

A Perfect Storm of Factors Sap[2] World Food Supply

WHEAT 130%

SOYA 87%

RICE 74%

CORN 31%

数据来源：Bloomberg

图片提供：Reuters 达志

CNN ANCHOR

Now, all this week we're taking a close-up look at the global food crisis. The United Nations is calling for urgent and concerted[3] action to prevent a global humanitarian[4] disaster. Soaring food prices have already resulted in deadly violence in some countries, and some are saying it could get a lot worse. So why is all this happening now? Zain Verjee reports on what is being called a perfect storm.

ZAIN VERJEE, CNN CORRESPONDENT

Higher food prices spell disaster for the world's poorest—millions living under a dollar a day at risk.

Global Food Crisis

25-F.MP3
25-S.MP3

perfect storm
完美风暴

perfect storm 一词是记者 Sebastian Junger 在 1993 年所创，原本是指 1991 年加拿大大西洋沿岸一场罕见的高纬度热带风暴，一般称为 Halloween Nor' easter。因为各种气候条件齐备，风暴的威力出乎意料地强大，造成 12 人死亡及 2.08 亿美元损失。1997 年 Junger 写成 *The Perfect Storm* 一书，2000 年据此拍成的电影《天摇地动》让这个词汇大为流行。该词用来比喻"各种因素齐备而造成的大灾难"。

· Lack of clean drinking water and crowded living conditions created a **perfect storm** for an outbreak of disease.
干净饮水缺乏加上居住环境拥挤形成了疾病爆发的绝佳环境。

CNN 主播

我们这个星期要深入探究全球粮食危机。联合国正在号召紧急的协同行动，以避免全球性的人道灾难。粮价飙涨已经在部分国家导致严重的暴力行为，有些人说情况还可能更糟。为什么现在会一下子发生这么些事呢？洁茵·维尔吉带来以下报道，探讨这场所谓的完美风暴。

CNN 特派员 洁茵·维尔吉

节节高升的粮价对世界上最贫穷的人将是一场大灾难。每天生活费仅仅一美元的数百万人民正处于危机当中。

1. **cupboard** [ˈkʌbəd]
   n. 食橱；橱柜

2. **sap** [sæp] *v.* 消耗；削弱
   The thin mountain air sapped the climber's energy.

3. **concerted** [kənˈsɜːtɪd]
   adj. 多方配合的
   Geoff made a concerted effort to quite smoking.

4. **humanitarian** [hjuˌmænəˈtɛriən]
   adj. 人道主义的
   The United Nations flew humanitarian aid into the war-ravaged country.

行业之道
品牌哲学
财经内幕
商海拾趣
环球生活

CONDOLEZZA RICE, U.S. SECRETARY OF STATE

No one should have to spend all of their daily wages just to buy their daily bread.[5]

ZAIN VERJEE, CNN CORRESPONDENT

But in just one year, the price of corn has gone up 31 percent on global markets; rice, 74 percent; soya, 87 percent; wheat, 130 percent.

Walk down any aisle at a supermarket and you can see food prices are going up. In much of the western world, consumers are able to absorb[6] the impact, but for many in the developing world, food prices are a matter of life and death.

The World Food Programme's map of hardest-hit regions stretches from the Caribbean to Africa and Asia. It's a perfect storm of sudden changes. Record-high oil prices, fast-rising transportation and fertilizer[7] costs, bad weather destroying crops, plus rising demand in India and China, and increased production of ethanol[8] converting[9] food crops into fuel.

JEFFREY SACHS, SPECIAL U.N. ADVISER

You add it all together: demand is soaring; supply has been cut back; food has been diverted[10] into the gas tank—it's added up to[11] a price explosion.

美国国务卿 康道莉萨·赖斯

任何人都不该过着每日拿到的工资只够填饱肚子的生活。

CNN 特派员 洁茵·维尔吉

但才不到一年，全球市场的玉米价格就上涨了 31%，稻米 74%，大豆 87%，小麦 130%。

逛逛超市里任何一条通道，你就可以看出粮食价格不断上涨。在西方世界的大部分地区，消费者还吸收得了价格上涨的冲击，但对发展中世界的许多人而言，粮食价格却是生死攸关的事。

在世界粮食计划署的资料中，受害最深的地区从加勒比海一直到非洲与亚洲。这是一场由突然的改变而造成的完美风暴。油价创纪录、运输与肥料成本快速上涨、恶劣天气摧毁作物，加上印度与中国的需求增加，而且乙醇生产量提高，造成许多粮食作物被转成了燃料。

联合国特别顾问 杰弗里·萨克斯

把这一切因素加起来：需求飙升，供给减少，粮食被转变为燃料——这些因素加起来造成了价格的暴涨。

Notes & Vocabulary

a matter of life and death
生死攸关的事

matter 指"事情；问题"，a matter of life and death 则表示某事物非常重要，关乎生死存亡、成败得失。

· Timely delivery of the medical supplies is a matter of life and death.
能否及时配送医疗补给品，是生死攸关的事。

cut back
大幅削减

cut back 原本是指"修剪树枝"，另外常表示"大量删减某物"，如预算、开支、产量等，名词写为 cutback。

· The city government cut back spending to balance its annual budget.
市政府削减开支以平衡年度预算。

5. **daily bread** [ˈdelɪ] [brɛd]
   每日所需的食粮

6. **absorb** [əbˈsɔrb] *v.* 吸收；承担
   Surrounding communities absorbed residents of the flooded town.

7. **fertilizer** [ˈfɝtˌlaɪzə] *n.* 肥料

8. **ethanol** [ˈɛθəˌnol] *n.* 酒精；燃料

9. **convert** [kənˈvɝt] *v.* 转变；变换
   The engine converts kitchen grease to automotive fuel.

10. **divert** [dəˈvɝt] *v.* 使转向；转移
    The aqueduct diverts water from the river to several farms.

11. **add up to** 导致；结果
    An increase in foreclosures adds up to a drop in home prices.

行业之道 品牌哲学 财经内幕 商海拾趣 环球生活

CONDOLEZZA RICE, U.S. SECRETARY OF STATE

We clearly have twin problems. We have an energy problem and we have a food problem, and there are some relationships between them.

ZAIN VERJEE, CNN CORRESPONDENT

Half the world's food aid comes from the U.S., $1.5 billion a year, but the money's not going far.

HENRIETTA FORE, U.S. AGENCY FOR INTL., DEVELOPMENT

It means that … hmm … less food is going to almost every recipient[12] because the prices are so much higher. So our U.S. dollar purchasing power[13] cannot stretch[14] as far.

ZAIN VERJEE, CNN CORRESPONDENT

The U.N. World Food Programme feeds one cup of porridge to 20 million schoolchildren. And the director says, it's the only food most of them see all day.

JOSETTE SHEERAN, U.N. WORLD FOOD PROGRAMME

Today, I can fill this 40 percent less than I could last June. So it has a direct affect on us.

美国国务卿 康道丽萨·赖斯

我们显然面临着双重问题，一方面是能源问题，另一方面是粮食问题，而且这两者之间是互相关联的。

CNN 特派员 洁茵·维尔吉

世界半数的粮食援助来自美国，每年 15 亿美元。可是这笔钱的功效有限。

美国国际开发署 亨丽埃塔·福尔

意思就是说，几乎每个受援者所获得的粮食都减少了，因为现在的价格上涨了许多。因此，美元的购买力也不比以往。

CNN 特派员 洁茵·维尔吉

联合国世界粮食计划署为两千万名学童供应的粮食就是一杯粥。署长表示，大多数学童一整天的食物就是这么一杯粥。

联合国世界粮食计划署 乔塞特·希兰

和去年 6 月比较起来，我今天能够提供的粮食已经减少了 40%。所以，粮食问题对我们具有直接的影响。

Notes & Vocabulary

go far
非常成功；成效卓著
字面上是指"行远路；走得远"，引申为某事物"延续长久；够用"或"发挥长足效果"，或表示某人"成就非凡"的意思。

- With plenty of natural talent and persistence, Gina went far in the entertainment business.
吉娜拥有绝佳的天赋和才华，加上不懈的努力，她在演艺界最终成就非凡。

12. **recipient** [rɪˈsɪpiənt]
n. 接受者；受领者

13. **purchasing power** [ˈpɜtʃəsɪŋ] [pauə] 购买力

14. **stretch** [strɛtʃ]
v. 尽全力；竭尽所能
The office stretched its staff resources to meet the new deadline.

行业之道 品牌哲学 财经内幕 商海拾趣 环球生活

ZAIN VERJEE, CNN CORRESPONDENT

The World Bank is calling for $500 million in emergency donations.[15]

ROBERT ZOELLICK, PRESIDENT, WORLD BANK

We can't afford to wait. We have to put our money where our mouth is now, so that we can put food into hungry mouths.

ZAIN VERJEE, CNN CORRESPONDENT

More cash may be a fast fix only in the short term, still leaving the hungry to fight for what little food there is, and security forces being drafted[16] in to guard not banks, but warehouses of food.

25-F.MP3 / 25-S.MP3 ▌ *The Cupboard Is Bare*

CNN 特派员 洁茵·维尔吉

世界银行正在募集 5 亿美元的紧急捐款。

世界银行总裁 罗伯·佐里克

我们没有本钱等待。我们必须身体力行，才能够把食物送入饥饿的嘴巴。

CNN 特派员 洁茵·维尔吉

多一点现金只能是在短期内立即见效的药方，饥饿的民众还是必须争抢仅有的少数粮食，征召来的安全部队不是为了看守银行，而是为了看护粮仓。

Notes & Vocabulary

put one's money where one's mouth is

身体力行；说到做到

字面意思是"把钱放到嘴巴所在的地方"，其实是表示用实际行动达到所说的理想，即中文"身体力行；说到做到"。

· If people are really interested in helping the earthquake victims, they should put their money where their mouth is.
如果人们真的有意帮助地震灾民，就应该身体力行。

15. **donation** [do`neʃən]
    n. 捐款；捐赠

16. **draft** [dræft] v. 征召；征集
    The NBA team drafted several promising college players.

行业之道 | 品牌哲学 | 财经内幕 | 商海拾趣 | 环球生活

Too Hot to Handle?

Opponents[1] Give Global Warming the Cold Shoulder

JOE JOHNS, CORRESPONDENT

For the most part, Al Gore was preaching[2] his gospel[3] of global warming to the already converted.[4]

Al GORE, FORMER U.S. VICE PRESIDENT

The planet has a fever. If your baby has a fever, you go to the doctor. If the doctor says, "You need to intervene[5] here," you don't say, "Well, I read a science fiction novel that tells me it's not a problem."

26-F.MP3
26-S.MP3

Notes & Vocabulary

标题扫描

give sb. the cold shoulder
cold shoulder 在这里不是指冷肩膀，而是 "忽略；不理睬"。因此 give sb. the cold shoulder 是 "对某人冷冷的或是刻意忽略" 的意思。

- Walter's ex-girlfriend gave him the cold shoulder at the party.
  瓦特的前女友在派对上刻意不理他。

CNN 特派员 乔・约翰
戈尔多半时候都在向已经改变了想法的人们反复重申全球变暖的道理。

前美国副总统 戈尔
地球现在发烧了。如果你的婴儿发烧了，你会去看医生。如果医生说："你得立刻想点办法。" 你不会说："我读了一本科幻小说，书上说发烧没什么关系。"

1. **opponent** [əˋponənt]
   n. 对手；敌手；反对者

2. **preach** [pritʃ] *v.* 鼓吹；反复灌输
   Jocelyn preached the benefits of recycling to her coworkers.

3. **gospel** [ˋgɑspl]
   n. 信条；准则；真理

4. **convert** [kənˋvɜt]
   v. 使改变信仰或想法
   Sylvia converted her husband to the idea of buying a hybrid car.

5. **intervene** [ˌɪntəˋvin]
   v. 介入；调停
   Brenda intervened in a dispute between her sisters.

行业之道　品牌哲学　财经内幕　商海拾趣　环球生活